EMBLEMS
OF THE
INFINITE
KING

J. RYAN LISTER (PhD, The Southern Baptist Theological Seminary) is Professor of Theology at Western Seminary in Portland, Oregon, and director of doctrine and discipleship for Humble Beast.

ANTHONY M. BENEDETTO is an award-winning illustrator, and designer, working in a variety of mediums and genres. He is the cofounder of Nova Nimbus, a multidisciplinary creative studio in Portland, Oregon, that has worked with clients such as Adidas, Red Bull, and Humble Beast. He and his wife have four children.

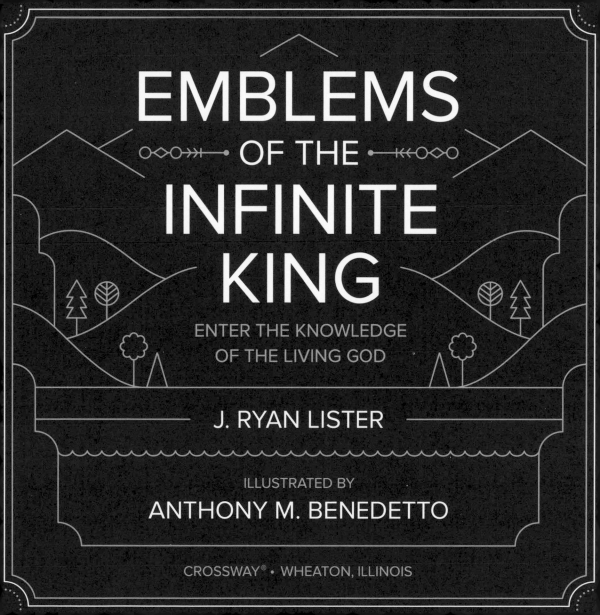

EMBLEMS
OF THE
INFINITE
KING

ENTER THE KNOWLEDGE
OF THE LIVING GOD

J. RYAN LISTER

ILLUSTRATED BY

ANTHONY M. BENEDETTO

CROSSWAY® • WHEATON, ILLINOIS

J. RYAN LISTER:

To Jude, Silas, Abby Kate, and Asher

May your infinite King give you eyes to see his glory, ears to hear his gospel,
a heart for him to dwell in, hands to serve him and be obedient to him,
and a mouth to sing his praises.

Forever.

ANTHONY M. BENEDETTO:

To Guvey Go-vee-vees, Lovies, Bogie Bogini, and Griffiti

I love you so much it hurts my heart. You see dimly now,
but even the smallest glimpse of God's beauty can change everything.
I pray he opens your eyes to see it.

Emblems of the Infinite King: Enter the Knowledge of the Living God

Copyright © 2019 by J. Ryan Lister

Illustrations © 2019 by Anthony M. Benedetto

Published by Crossway
        1300 Crescent Street
        Wheaton, Illinois 60187

Illustrations and book design by Anthony M. Benedetto, Nova Nimbus

Cover design & illustration: Anthony M. Benedetto

First printing 2019

Printed in China

Scripture quotations are from the ESV® Bible (*The Holy Bible, English Standard Version®*), copyright © 2001 by Crossway, a publishing ministry of Good News Publishers. Used by permission. All rights reserved.

Thank you to Justin Taylor for his "who and what" helpful illustration of the Trinity (p. 32).
See "Explaining the Trinity to a Seven-Year-Old," The Gospel Coalition website, October 15, 2010,
https://www.thegospelcoalition.org/blogs/justin-taylor/explaining-the-trinity-to-a-seven-year-old/.

Hardcover ISBN: 978-1-4335-6338-6
ePub ISBN: 978-1-4335-6341-6
PDF ISBN: 978-1-4335-6339-3
Mobipocket ISBN: 978-1-4335-6340-9

Library of Congress Cataloging-in-Publication Data

Names: Lister, J. Ryan (John Ryan), 1978– author. | Benedetto, Anthony M., 1982–
    illustrator.

Title: Emblems of the infinite king : enter the knowledge of the living God / J. Ryan
    Lister and Anthony M. Benedetto.

Description: Wheaton, Illinois : Crossway, [2019] | Audience: Ages 8–14. | Includes
    bibliographical references.

Identifiers: LCCN 2018055678 (print) | LCCN 2019011010 (ebook) | ISBN
    9781433563393 (pdf) | ISBN 9781433563409 (mobi) | ISBN 9781433563416
    (epub) | ISBN 9781433563386 (hbk.) | ISBN 9781433563416 (epub)

Subjects: LCSH: Christianity—Juvenile literature. | Theology, Doctrinal—Juvenile
    literature.

Classification: LCC BR125.5 (ebook) | LCC BR125.5 .L57 2019 (print) |
    DDC 246/.5—dc23

LC record available at https://lccn.loc.gov/2018055678

Crossway is a publishing ministry of Good News Publishers.

RRD   29 28 27 26 25 24 23 22 21 20 19
15 14 13 12 11 10 9 8 7 6 5 4 3 2 1

CONTENTS

PICK UP THE KEY AND OPEN THE LOCK

His strong and wise command cut through the empty silence
as he reached out of the shadows to offer an ancient key.

"I am the Key Keeper. I have come to show you
the Way. But before you do anything . . .

"Heed this warning:

"Those who turn this key will never be the same.

"It will show your deepest guilt and display your darkest shame.

"You'll see who you were made to be and what you've really become.

"But only if you turn the key will you find your story isn't done, that the way ahead is the path that leads into the throne room of the Son, this one they call the Death Killer, who gives his life to pay your ransom.

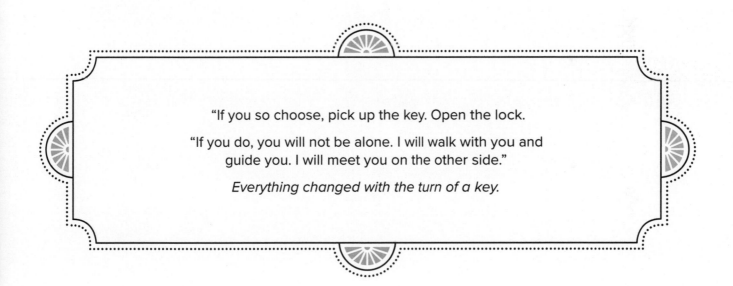

"If you so choose, pick up the key. Open the lock.

"If you do, you will not be alone. I will walk with you and guide you. I will meet you on the other side."

Everything changed with the turn of a key.

THE THRONE ROOM KEY

As you turn the key, a door opens into a room made out
of the heavens. Above, there is a canopy built out of stars
whose light curves down to form the most brilliant floor
you've ever seen. In the middle of the room sits a throne
holding a figure so bright, he seems to be wearing the sun,
or maybe he is the very source of every light ever known.

You desperately want to look away, but you can't. His beauty
and glory calm your fears and somehow, at the same time,
make you more afraid. You don't know what to do, where
to turn, or how you can stand before him much longer.

But that's when you hear the Key Keeper.

That's when that wise voice—the same one that offered
you the key—whispers in your ear and explains . . .

THE THRONE ROOM'S SONG

YOUR STORY BEGINS WITH A SONG

our story begins with a song. It is a simple song. No verse. Just a chorus. But it rings like thunder in your ears. No song in human history has ever come close to its terrifying beauty, because it's like no other song ever written. This one was composed for someone who actually deserves it, one bigger than the world, one different from everyone and everything else you've ever known or could know.

This song is fit only for a king. But not just any king.

This song belongs to the King of kings. The one seated on the throne in front of you. It is for him and him alone. Only the Creator, the Lord and Ruler of all, is worthy of this chorus. It is why he creates angels of fire to sing its majestic words. It is why music exists in the first place. It is why this song echoes throughout this heavenly throne room around you, and it is why everything he created has this song written on their hearts:

> *Holy, holy, holy is the LORD of hosts;*
> *the whole earth is full of his glory! (Isa. 6:3)*

You can hear it now, can't you? The King made everything in the world to sing this song—with their voices and with their lives.

That includes you. He made you to sing his chorus. This is why your story starts *here*. In *his* throne room. With *his* song.

Because every story starts here.

Because every story starts with the King.

KNOWLEDGE OF THE KING

YOUR STORY IS NOT ALL ABOUT YOU

is song makes one thing crystal clear: your story is not really *your* story. The King made the world to sing *his* glory, and he made you to sing *his* song.

This may be a little confusing at first. We all want to be the main character in our own story. Everybody—in his own way—wants to be the center of his world. Everyone wants to be king of the mountain, the smartest kid in the class, the one with the biggest trophy case, or everybody's best friend. It hurts when you aren't and, after a while, it can even hurt when you are.

This is why knowing the King is so important. Knowing him shows you that you can't be the center of the world *because he already is*. That is a good thing. You weren't made to be the center of the world; you can't hold everything together. But God can. And when he is the center of the world, and the center of your story, you are free to be who you were made to be—who *he* made you to be.

Knowing God is like finally finding the lost box top to the thousand-piece puzzle you've been working on for two weeks. Now that you know what this puzzle is supposed to look like, you can stop guessing. Knowing God makes sense of things—you don't have to try to make things work on your own. When God is your King, the strange and messy things in this world and in your life actually start fitting together. Knowing God puts things in their right place.

That is why knowing the King is the most important thing about you. What you think and feel about God defines who you are, where you are going, what gives you hope, and what makes you *really* happy.

THE KING'S SPEECH

THE KING WANTS YOU TO KNOW HIM

I f knowing the King is really the most important thing, then you need to know him correctly. This is where it gets really good: God doesn't play hide-and-seek with you. He actually comes to you. The King *wants* you to know him, and, in his kind mercy, he has actually already spoken to you in many ways.

You can find his speech, first, in his creation. Like painters who sign their paintings, God's signature is everywhere in the world he designed. Everything he made points you back to him as the Maker. You hear it in heaven's song. God's creation sings his glory and tells you about his endless power and divine ways.

The King also speaks to you through your conscience. Your conscience is that voice in your head that tells you when something is right or wrong. God made you so you could tell the difference between good and evil. It's why you feel bad when you do bad things and good when you do good things. That is because God made you this way. He made you to want the good because he made you to desire him, and he is the best good we could ever find.

Both nature outside (creation) and your nature inside (conscience) tell every person ever created the truth about who God is and who you are. It even shows you how you've offended him and that you have no excuse for your guilt.

But by his grace, God isn't done speaking. He doesn't just speak in general ways. Yes, he speaks through the works of his hands and the law he writes on your heart, but he also draws near to his world to talk to you. He speaks to you in a special way with a special message about the King's special project to save you from your guilt. Long ago at many times and in many ways, God spoke in this special way through his prophets. He used dreams and visions, and even visibly appeared to his people in order to show them how they might know him well once again. All of these special words and ways point forward to something better, though—some*one* better. The King speaks in a very special way when he tells you about and gives the world his greatest Word—his Son, Jesus Christ—the one he sent into your world in order to save it.

And how do you know this? God wrote it down. He wanted you to be able to hear him speak any time you read his words, what those in your world call the Bible. In both the Old and New Testaments of Scripture, God works with the words, lives, and qualities of human authors to give you his perfect words—not just to have them, but so that you may believe and obey them and find life in them. The Bible is the King's way to knowing the King. It's his love letter to his lost children. It's his four-course meal for the poor and the hungry.

Because the King speaks through Scripture, you can trust it to be a perfect guide to knowing him. Every part of it is from God, which means it doesn't have any errors. It means you can understand it, and it means that it already contains everything God wants you to know. It also means that God will use it to make sure that what he wants to happen will indeed happen.

Now this is too important to miss, so listen well: the only real reason you can know the King is because the King *wants* you to know him. He tells you everything you need to know about him. Now, he doesn't tell you everything; but everything he *does* tell you is true and exactly what you need to know.

The King wants you to hear his words because he wants you to know him rightly. People will try to tell you who God is; but the truth is, God himself has already told you who he is. He's given you his Word. The question is, will you hear and heed his Word?

He wants you to hear it because he wants you to be happy. You see, God made these two things—knowing him and your happiness—to go together. He knows you will find your true, right, and perfect happiness only when you know the true, right, and perfect King.

He speaks to you so that you may sing his song.

THE "OTHER THAN" KING

YOU ARE NOT THE KING AND THE KING IS NOT YOU

his is where the knowledge of God begins; it is the lesson of the throne room and Scripture:

You are not the King, and the King is not you.

You don't know anyone like this King. He is bigger than you, not limited like you, beyond your control, and beyond your imagination. He is superior, infinite, and full of glory. As the Creator, he alone reigns over creation. And as *your* Creator, he reigns over you as well.

He is the "other than" King.

Knowing this puts everything in the right place. You belong to the King; it is not the other way around. He tells you who he is; it is not the other way around. He sits on the throne; it is not the other way around. You find your happiness in him; it is not the other way around.

One of the best ways to know God, in fact, is to know how he *outshines* you. Just think about this:

God is God because God is infinite.

God does not have limitations like you do. You are finite. You can't do everything; in fact, you have a hard enough time getting out of bed to get ready for school. It is different for the King, though. His power knows no bounds, and his control and rule extend to everything that belongs to him, which is . . . . well . . . everything. Nothing controls or restricts him either. Only God controls God, and he does so perfectly. This is why God cannot tell a lie. This is not a limitation of his ability; it is that his truthfulness has no limits. God cannot sin because God's perfect holiness is never-ending.

God is God because God needs no one and nothing.

But you do, right? God is perfectly happy in himself. He didn't create the world because he needed or wanted something. That would mean that he wasn't complete in himself—that there was something missing in God. Which would mean he wouldn't be the true King because this need would reign over him. But God didn't create you and everything else because he was lonely or he needed something from us. He creates for a bigger and better reason: love.

God is God because God is not limited by time and space.

But you are. You know that feeling you get when you wish you were somewhere else? Or maybe you've always wanted to be older? Or you wish you could go back and relive your favorite memory? You feel frustrated because of the limitations of time and space. God, though, never feels these frustrations or limitations. He created time and rules over it. He did the same for space and place. Which means time and space serve him, not the other way around.

God is God because God does not change like the rest of his creation.

But you do. If you think about your life, change is everywhere. Oceans have tides. Night follows day. Winter becomes spring. Change is why your grandparents say you've grown so much since the last time you saw them. Change is why you have chores: make up your bed, clean the bathroom, mow the lawn. You are constantly trying to put things back the way they used to be before they *changed*. You change on the inside too—for better or worse. But for God—who is outside of time and space and who is perfect perfection—there is no such thing as better or worse. Change is a part of his creation, but change is not a part of God's nature. He has been and always will be the same once-and-future King.

God is God because God doesn't have a beginning or end.

But you do. You've probably seen your baby pictures. It's when you joined your family, entered the world, and began your life. God is different from you, though. He doesn't have any baby pictures because God always was, is, and will be. It is his nature to exist. To be God is to always be. God did not come from something or someone else—if he had, he would cease to be God. He is the great "I Am," the King who reigns from eternity past to eternity future. He doesn't begin, and he certainly won't end. He doesn't enter the world, and he certainly won't exit it. He is before the world ever was, and he is the sole reason the world exists at all. He will be after the world, and he will be the sole reason the world is made new.

God is God because God is holy and worthy of glory.

But you are not. You are not holy, nor do you deserve his glory. God's holiness is very important. It is the focus of the King's throne room song, which sums up the King's character: he is holy, holy, holy. At its most basic, holiness means that the Lord is set apart from everything, including all of his creation. He is different from us. That means that his ways are different from our ways, but it also means that he is pure, good, and faultless, while you are not always these things. That is why he alone deserves praise. He alone deserves worship. He alone deserves all of you.

But perhaps the greatest difference between you and God is that he is a Trinity and you are not. Don't let this word scare you. It simply means that there is one God who has and always will exist in three persons: Father, Son, and Holy Spirit. Each person is fully God and each person is different from the others *and* there is only one God.

The Trinity is a big reason why God is the "other than" King. Even though the Trinity sometimes seems really hard to understand, that doesn't mean we shouldn't try. Remember, the King made you to sing his song; he wants you to know him *this* way. So to help, think about the difference between "who" and "what." Take the first president of the United States. If you were able to ask him the question, "Who are you?," he would answer, "George Washington." If you then asked him, "What are you?," he would likely respond, "Well, I'm a human being, of course."

Now what happens when we ask God the same questions? His answers would be a little like George Washington's but *a lot different* too. According to his own speech, God would answer like this:

Who are you? *The Father.* What are you? *The one God.*

Who are you? *The Son.* What are you? *The one God.*

Who are you? *The Spirit.* What are you? *The one God.*

The King's answers highlight the beauty of the Trinity. While God is perfectly three persons (that *who* question we asked), he—at the same time—still has only one nature (that *what* question). God is the perfect three "who's" and one "what." God's three persons-in-one-nature makes him worthy of worship. God is completely happy in the Trinity; that is why he needs nothing besides himself. While we need others to help us and take care of us, God doesn't. The King has a perfect "three-in-one" relationship that makes him happy and filled with joy.

This is what he calls love.

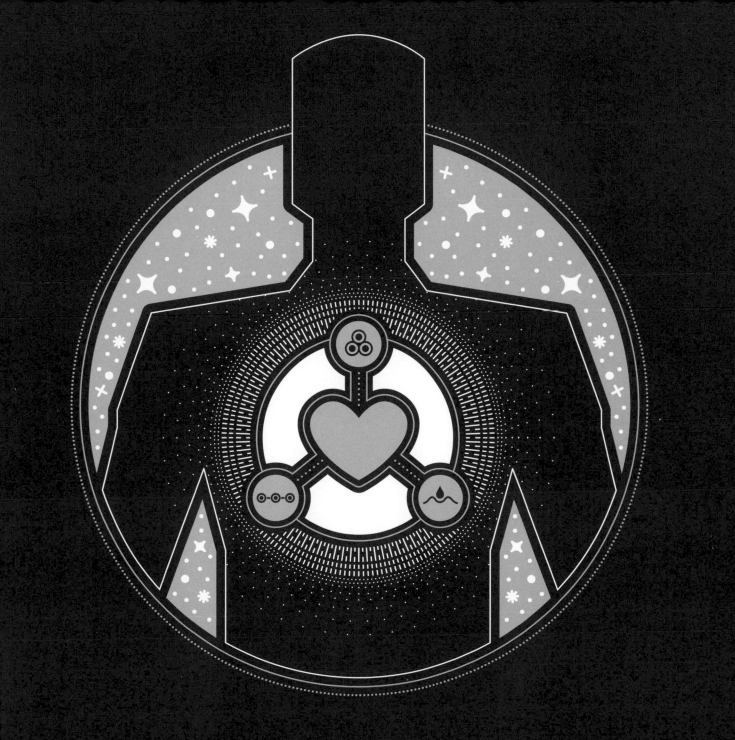

THE "WITH YOU" KING

GOD'S LOVE IS IN EVERYTHING HE DOES

**B**ut this inside-the-Trinity love—the love the Father, Son, and Spirit have for one another—is so big and so perfect that it spills over into everything God does and everything he has made. This is the beauty of the "other than" King. His "other-than-ness" frees him to do whatever he pleases and, for him, it pleases him to draw near to you. Because God is the "other than" King, he can also be the "with you" King.

Why else would he speak to you? Why else would I offer you his key?

Remember the throne room song's second line: "The whole earth is full of his glory." While the first line tells you about God's greatness, the second line tells you that everything knows he is great. This means that the King didn't just create the world; he enters into his world to speak to you and to know you. The "other than" King who sits on a throne in heaven is also the "with you" King who walks in the world he made and talks with the creatures he created.

In order to be the "with you" King, God shares a few of his qualities with you so that you can know him better. This doesn't mean that you are God or are able to become him; instead, it means that God made you to reflect his character to his world in a limited way. God made you to have wisdom, love, goodness, faithfulness, mercy, patience, justice, righteousness, and grace. You have these qualities only partially and imperfectly; your King, on the other hand, has them in full, without limitations. Still, you are like God in this: you mirror the King's character to the King's world in a way that helps you know him and enjoy him and that calls others who can see his faint reflection in you to do the same.

SING THE KING'S CHORUS

LISTEN TO GOD AND FOLLOW HIS WORDS

od made you to know him, which is why knowing him is the most important thing about you. He made you not just to know about him but to really, personally *know* him.

To do this, you must listen to him and follow his words. You will be tempted to write your own story. You will be tempted to try to write the King's story for him. You will want to control him even though you cannot. You will even be tempted to try to take his place.

Perhaps you already have. Have you ever thought that God should do things the way *you* want him to do them? Have you ever thought to yourself, "I could do a lot of this better than God"? Have you ever been mad at God because he doesn't listen to you when you tell him how to run your life?

That is why the throne room's lesson is so important. Remember: you are not the King, and the King is not you.

That is why your story begins with a song.

If you want to sing this song rightly, if you want to know where your song leads, turn the next key.

And open the lock.

With a turn of the key, the stars and throne disappear. Everything goes black; his song goes silent. This is a different darkness, unlike any you've ever felt before.

There is nothing but nothing before your eyes. Everything you've ever known, everything you thought would always be there—the sky, the sun, grass, color, wind, gravity, laughter, air—is gone. All that stands before you is void and darkness. The emptiness feels unbearable; you just want to go back to the way things used to be. But there is nowhere to turn because there is no "where."

Just before panic sets in, a new, severe, and regal voice cuts through the dark with a direct command.

"Let there be light."

And just as that last word echoes in the void, a burst of brilliant white overcomes the darkness.

But the speaker is not done. With more words comes more creation: "Let there be a heaven, earth, and sea. Let the earth bring forth plants, fruits, and trees. Let the sky be filled with the sun, moon, and stars, and let them divide day from night. Let the seas, the earth, and the sky be filled with wildlife." And in just a few sentences, everything you once knew and took for granted—night and day, earth and sky—was back and better than it ever was.

That's when you see him. Like a conductor before his newly made orchestra, the King stands watching and directing the world his words have brought into existence.

Everything already seemed perfect and right, but the King is building up to his finale. He even changes his approach. Instead of speaking something new into existence like before, this time, he slows down and lets you listen in on his divine plans:

"Let us make man in our image, after our likeness."

These simple words seem like a map to buried treasure. They are the King's answer to the world's biggest, most important questions. By making humanity in his own likeness, God gives your life beauty, order, and purpose. Having the image of God explains who you are, why you matter, and what your life is really all about.

But what does it mean to be made in the image of the King? Where do you even begin to understand this?

That's when you hear that familiar wise voice behind you whisper . . .

THE IMAGE BEARERS' BEGINNING

YOUR PURPOSE LIES IN THE DUST

Your purpose lies in the dust.

As God's Word tells you, the "LORD God formed the man of dust from the ground" (Gen 2:7).

You won't find this in your school's science textbooks, and it won't be the lead story on the evening news. Nobody wants to trace their beginnings back to a clod of dirt or lump of clay. It's not glamorous, and it certainly doesn't fit with the world's "you can be anything you want to be" promises.

That's why humanity works so hard to forget its humble beginnings. Even you will try to forget where you came from.

But God's way is better than yours. He is the Creator. He's the Creator of everything. Including you. He knows how all things work and how all things work together. Including you. The King wrote your owner's manual. Which is good, because if the world worked your way, it would probably turn out like sandcastles built beside the sea—small kingdoms we make that are quickly washed away by the incoming tide.

This is why God's perspective on your humanity is so important. When he tells you your beginning, he helps you see where you should go. It's like planning for a trip. To get where you want to go, you have to know where your journey starts. The beginning and the end always connect, and they help make sense of all the points along the way too.

When you know that God is your sculptor and you are his clay, you know how your story starts. You know that you are under God's reign. God created you in ways beyond your imagination—ways that spotlight his power, authority, and wisdom—to show you that he rules over you and that you rely on him. You didn't make yourself; God did. The dirt under your feet should be a constant reminder that you owe your life—your everything—to your King.

The dust you came from should also remind you that being a human means that, like the earth's dirt, you are real and physical.

You aren't some ghostlike life force floating around in the atmosphere. You have a real body with real arms and feet and hands and a nose. You live in a physical world that you can touch, taste, hear, see, and smell.

And when your King fashions you out of the earth, he forever connects you to the rest of his creation. Though humanity and the world aren't the same thing, your stories intertwine. Try to think of your life without the sky above and the earth beneath. It's impossible and, as the void and the darkness showed you, it's unbearable. Man and the world are in this together. That's why, as you will soon see, when the first man rebels against the King, the King punishes him *and* the world. The King turns the once fruitful and thriving creation into thorns and thistles. Yet, in his grace, when the King promises to rescue humanity, he promises to rescue the world too.

God also creates humanity out of dust to show you that you are the high point of creation. Now this may sound odd at first. God speaks everything else into existence—making things out of nothing—but man he forms out of something else: dirt. That doesn't sound like man is the pinnacle of God's creation, does it?

But that's the point. God makes humanity differently than the way he makes the rest of creation because he makes the rest of creation *for* humanity. It's like getting to the theater before the play begins. The stage is set and ready for the performance. But you didn't come to see the set design; you came to see the actors bring that stage to life. The set isn't the story; it exists to help tell the actors' story. It is the same with God's design. The world is the stage he builds to tell the story about his relentless love for humanity. That is why the King makes the world first, then the man and the woman, and then he plants them in his perfect garden.

The King builds a place for his people so he can be present with his people.

THE IMAGE BEARERS' WAYS

THERE IS MORE TO HUMANITY THAN DIRT

hat is why there is more to your humanity than just dirt.

There is the breath of God also. To make man a living creature, the King actually "breathed into [Adam's] nostrils the breath of life, and the man became a living creature" (Gen. 2:7). While he speaks the rest of creation into existence from afar, the King makes man in a close, "face-to-face" way.

This two-part creation of man—earth and breath—hints at this truth: the King made you with two unified parts. First, the King gave you a physical body. Remember, God used the real, physical world to create the first man. But there is also the second part—a spiritual or soul part—found in the breath of life the King breathed into humanity.

These two parts work to make up one whole. Adam is not completely Adam without both the physical and spiritual parts united together in him. That is why he isn't a living creature until he has both. Body and soul work together like a harmony. They are two notes played at the same time to make a beautiful and more striking sound together. Or it's like playing a chord on a piano or a guitar. You press two different keys or strings to make one note. If you miss a key or a string, then it is no longer a chord.

It is the same with your humanity. To be human is to have both body and soul. It was that way with the first man, and it is that way with you right now.

THE IMAGE OF GOD

THE REASON WHY HE MADE YOU

ut God doesn't just tell you what you're made of, he actually stops—in the middle of his creation project—to explain *why* he made you in the first place. In the simplest terms, God creates you to image him in his world. As his Word puts it, "God created man in his own image, in the image of God he created him; male and female he created them" (Gen. 1:27).

This simple sentence helps answer so many of the questions about what it means to be human. While all the philosophers, teachers, and thinkers of this world try so hard to give you deep complex answers about your humanity, the King just tells you, "This is what I made you to be." In this brief moment, when the King lets you hear his "inside-the-Trinity" reason for creating you, everything begins to make sense.

When God said, "Let us make man in our image, after our likeness," he really meant it and he really did it (Gen. 1:26). He made humanity to reflect his character and his ways to the watching world. The King created a creature who would be "like" him, a creature who would represent the King in the King's world.

In a way, then, humanity is like a flag. Just like a flag represents a country's rule and reign wherever it flies, you represent and reflect God's rule and reign in his creation. A flag on its own is just colorful fabric; its power and purpose come only from the country it stands for. Like the flag, your power and purpose come from the King who made you to represent him in his world. When creation sees you, it sees an ambassador of the King, one who reflects his rule, power, and authority on the King's behalf.

THE IMAGE BEARERS' PURPOSE

GOD CREATED YOU TO REPRESENT THE KING

ou bear God's image for a *purpose*. God creates you in his image to represent the King in who you are and what you do.

That is what it means to be made in the image and the likeness of the King.

So while man and woman reflect God in who they are, they also reflect God in their actions. That is why God gives the first man and woman two commands right after he makes them in his image. If they do these things, they reflect God to the rest of his creation.

So what are these commands and what do they have to do with the image of God? First, God tells his image bearers to "be fruitful and multiply and fill the earth." And second, God tells them to "have dominion over the fish of the sea and over the birds of the heavens and over every living thing that moves on the earth" (Gen. 1:28).

Think about what God commands you to do here. He wants you to grow in numbers and rule over every created thing. God is telling you to build his kingdom and oversee it for him.

That is why you are supposed "to be fruitful and multiply . . . and have dominion." Through the commands, the King connects his image with the expansion of his rule. Being fruitful and multiplying is God's way of telling his image bearers to make more image bearers. This is why God made you for relationships and why he made both males and females in his image. It's also why you exist, and your parents before you, and your grandparents before them. It's why Adam and Eve aren't the only people in God's world.

One person became two people, and they became a lot more people who then turned into a nation and so on. This is why your Bible has so many long lists of strange names. The King wants you to know that his image bearers are filling his world.

While God's image bearers grow in numbers, the borders of God's rule must expand as well. More people means you need more land, and as God's image bearers spread into the rest of God's world, God's kingdom rule goes with them. That is why the King wants you to "have dominion." God made you in his image to help you make sure that his rule and reign grow, flourish, and expand across all the world through you.

Eden is a little picture of this. It starts as a perfect garden the Creator gives his image bearers to practice their kingdom rule and enjoy his presence. But Eden was just supposed to be the beginning. If Adam and Eve kept God's commands, the beauty of Eden—this little kingdom—would extend over all the earth. Paradise would be worldwide. If the first couple had followed the King's commands and been who the King made them to be, they would have had all of the King's promises and found the King and his ways to be their highest joy.

A BETTER IMAGE BEARER

BECAUSE THE WORLD ISN'T PARADISE

ut the world isn't paradise. You are miles away from Eden. And so many people seem miles away from real joy, don't they?

That is because something bad happened. The world doesn't want God's kingdom anymore.

These days the image of God seems like a broken, fractured mirror with lots of missing pieces. Here's the problem: when people don't know who they are or what they're supposed to do, they make up their own answers and their own reasons. That's like trying to replace the sun with the moon. The moon isn't strong enough to keep things in orbit, and the planets would spin wildly out of control. You and your answers aren't strong enough either. You can't make up a purpose strong enough to keep your world together. Eventually it will spin out of control unless the King returns to his rightful place at its center.

In God's grace, he offers to restore your world. God promises to piece back together again the image you fractured by doing the unimaginable. God becomes man to show you the perfect image of God. God the Son enters the world as the man Christ Jesus. He becomes a better Adam to fix what the first Adam broke. Christ reteaches you who you're supposed to be and what you're supposed to do. In the Son, you have a way to be truly, fully human once again.

Only the King's kingdom lasts. This is why he made you for his kingdom and tied your life to it. It's also why you need God's Son to restore you to his kingdom.

But before you can fully understand how Christ rescues your humanity, you must first feel a different kind of darkness. Not the "before-creation" darkness you felt when you turned this key, but the darkness that enters the world through a serpent's fork-tongued lies.

If you are ready—if you have the courage to face the darkness of your sin and death—turn this key and open the lock.

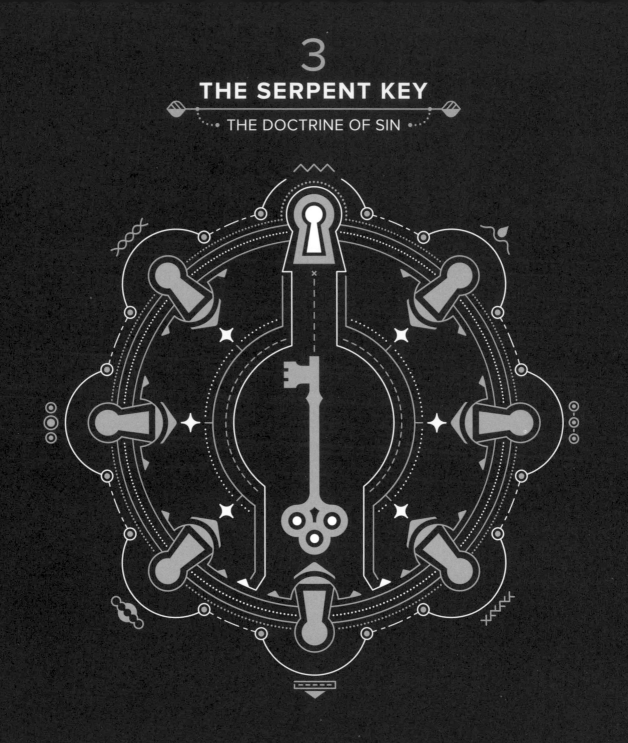

3
THE SERPENT KEY
THE DOCTRINE OF SIN

You turn the key, and the young cosmos gives way to a perfect garden. It's like a dream. No plant is out of place, no tree limb is too long, and no flower petal is missing. Everything you've ever wanted or needed seems to be within reach. For the first time you feel perfectly content. You are calm and happy to be exactly where you are. You can't even think of anywhere you'd rather be. It's like being on a long, long journey and finally getting back home.

That is until you hear that wise and familiar voice behind you say . . .

THE ORIGINS OF SIN

YOUR PROBLEM BEGINS WITH A SERPENT

our problem begins with a serpent.

The serpent wanted the King's throne but soon realized he wasn't powerful enough to bring the King down. The King was and is too perfect, too holy, too loving, and too happy within himself. Nothing could pull God off course. He would have his divine way, no matter how hard the snake tried.

Yet the serpent found what he thought to be a loophole—a mistake—in God's plan (you will soon learn that the perfect King makes no mistakes).

That "mistake," according to the serpent, was Adam and his beautiful wife, Eve.

The first couple was everything the serpent hated about the King. The King made them beautiful, innocent, and satisfied with the King and his blessings. He planted them in Eden, a lush garden, and then gave them the keys to his paradise. The King loved Adam and Eve. The High and Holy One would even step off his throne to serve, love, and draw near to his creation.

Even more, the King designed Adam and Eve to reflect his image to the rest of the world. He made them to rule over his creation. He created them to find their utmost joy in worshiping, experiencing, and loving him above all things.

The King had given Adam and Eve everything. He gave the first couple his world, and he gave them their purpose in his world. Everything was theirs, with one condition: they must not eat from the death-giving tree of the knowledge of good and evil.

This rule was not an empty threat or a cruel joke. It was a reminder. As strange as it may seem, this rule shows us that God is the world's greatest joy, not the gifts the King has so freely given.

The fruit was good, but the Creator and Sustainer of the fruit was better. The King set this rule to align our lives with him so that we may know him rightly and enjoy his gifts in light of who he is.

One thing is for sure: this condition, this moral requirement, this off-limits tree was the devil's way in. The tree was a way to demonstrate obedience and hope in the King, but the snake could ruin it all if he could make Adam do the opposite. The tree and its tempting fruit could drive a nail into Adam and Eve's relationship with their King and, with Adam gone, perhaps, just perhaps, the serpent could slither his way onto the King's throne.

It was a long shot, but the serpent was willing to risk it. Adam and Eve were not *exactly* like their King, which might make them vulnerable enough to fall under the snake's dark enchantment. In an ironic twist that only a snake could love, the serpent commenced his terrorist plot. If the serpent could just get the first man to reject his Creator as King, then the serpent could break the world from Eden to its edges.

The serpent slinked into God's perfect garden and began his assault in the shadows near the forbidden tree. He found his first victim. Just outside the darkness stood Eve, in her God-made beauty. His first step: subvert God's very good design by targeting Eve first, then Adam. Though Adam was the representative of all of humanity—and if he broke, the rest of creation would too—the serpent knew a full frontal attack on Adam would fail. But Eve's beauty and love could make the bitterest fruit sweet to Adam's taste.

It was time. The serpent stepped out of the shadows into Eve's gaze. Immediately, he was struck by how much the King's image was etched in her. He felt the painful reminder that—no matter how hard he tried—he would never escape the King, especially in the King's kingdom. Everything bore his divine fingerprints; everything sang of his glory.

Yet what was supposed to stir worship now just gave rise to hate. Standing before Eve, he realized that he hated Adam and Eve almost as much as he hated the King. Almost.

He hated that they were different; that they were innocent; that God cared for them so much; that they blindly obeyed their King; that they found rest in his love; that they reflected his beauty; that they received so much from him; that they took it all for granted; and that they ruled over everything, none of which was their own.

He restrained himself and calmly poured all of this anger into his first poisonous question for Eve:

"Did your King *really* tell you that you couldn't eat from this tree?"

Eve stumbled. This was the first foreign voice she had heard outside of Adam's and her Creator's, and it was questioning everything that she thought was unquestionable. Unaware of the war the serpent just waged against her and her King, she answered with a clarification:

"We can eat from every tree in the garden except the one that we are not supposed to even touch."

But her answer betrayed her. Eve didn't run from the deceiver; she tried to answer him. Eve didn't seek Adam's help; she answered *for* him instead. Eve didn't speak about God personally; she only talked about his gifts in light of his command.

Eve set out to correct the serpent: the King was not withholding *everything* from her, just the tree that led to certain death. Yet instead of correction, she made a way for sin to enter the world.

She had fallen into the trap. She engaged in debate with him, she forgot her husband and their union, and she began to see only the King's gifts—especially those she couldn't have—rather than the King himself.

A little more poison: if the serpent could just get Eve to believe him rather than her King.

"Oh, Eve, you will surely not die. Rather, your King knows that when you eat from this tree your eyes will finally be opened."

And then the final injection:

"When you eat from this tree *you will be like God.*"

There it was. The serpent had done it. He used the beautiful differences between the King and his image bearers to fracture the world. Even though Adam and Eve shined with God's image and were more like God than anything in all of the King's creation, both were ready to trade their King and his paradise for the fruit and its little lies. The outlawed tree's fruit was all that was good, beautiful, and true to Eve, and she gave in.

"Eve took of its fruit and ate, and she gave some to her husband who was with her, and he ate."

Two for one. Just as planned, Eve did the dirty work and got Adam to eat the fruit. As the representative of all humanity, Adam's sin fractured his life and the entire world, then and there and here and now. With a pinch of temptation, a dash of persuasion, and a pile of deceit, the serpent sweet-talked Adam and Eve into giving up everything they needed for the one thing they never did. They sold their legacy, birthright, future, purpose, hope, dream, peace, and innocence for a bite of forbidden fruit.

THE STAIN OF SIN

POISON POURED INTO THE GARDEN

**P**oison poured out into the garden and the rest of creation. But don't be fooled. The poison didn't come from the fruit; it came from Adam. It wasn't that God's gifts weren't enough for Adam. It was that God wasn't enough for Adam. The fruit wasn't off-limits because it could kill; it was off-limits because it offered godlike knowledge *without* God.

In taking the fruit, Adam, in a way, tried to pickpocket God, all while forgetting that God had already given him everything in his entire kingdom.

The serpent was right about *one thing*: everything changed. What was once right now seemed wrong. What was once false now seemed true. New feelings flooded into Adam and Eve. Anger churned, tears burned, relationships broke, grief and shame crushed. Everything had changed. But for the worse. Adam's sin messed up everything.

Not only for him, *but for you too*.

Adam's story helps you understand your own story. Adam's story shows you why you don't always get along with your brother or sister or friends. It is why you get angry with your parents sometimes. It explains why you feel sad and why you cry (even if you're good at hiding your tears).

Adam wasn't just the first man, or your first ancestor; he was also your representative before God. This means that whatever Adam did in the garden would affect everyone who followed him, including *you*. So when Adam chose to rebel against God, every human—everyone carrying the beautiful image of God—was stained by Adam's sin.

Adam is not just a warning or a bad example that you shouldn't follow. He isn't just another myth about how the world begins and why it feels so wrong all the time. His story isn't some lesson your parents made up to get you to obey them and eat your vegetables. No, Adam was real and so was his disobedience. He rebelled against the King in the very good garden and seared his heart and the hearts of all image bearers after him with sin. Adam's disease plagues everyone and everything to this very day.

Everyone and everything.

Just ask Cain and Abel. Ask Noah and his sons. Ask the architects of Babel's tower. Ask Moses and Joshua. And Israel's judges. Ask her prophets. And her priests. And her kings.

And if you still don't think that Adam's sin has anything to do with you, then just ask the apostle Paul. He holds up a mirror to us when he writes, "Just as sin came into the world through one man [Adam], and death through sin, and so death spread to all men because all sinned" (Rom. 5:12). Sin is *the* problem everyone must face because, as Paul writes, "all . . . are under sin, as it is written: 'None is righteous, no, not one; no one understands; no one seeks for God'" (Rom. 3:9–11).

And if you don't believe Paul, just go ahead and ask your parents. Ask them if they have any regrets or guilt or shame or if they have ever been wronged or wronged someone else. If they are honest—which is sometimes hard for us to be (another example of sin)—you will probably have a very long conversation.

But you don't even need to ask anyone really, do you? You probably already know sin personally. Has sin ever crept up on you? Have you ever felt pride and anger burn you up from the inside? Have you ever wondered why you don't always get along with your family? Or have you ever done something you knew you weren't supposed to do? Have you ever cringed because you relate better to the bad guys in your favorite books or movies?

This is because Adam's sin stained your heart. You carry the sin "disease" Adam passed on to you. This is one of the greatest results of sin: not only does your sin make you a sinner, but you sin *because* you're a sinner.

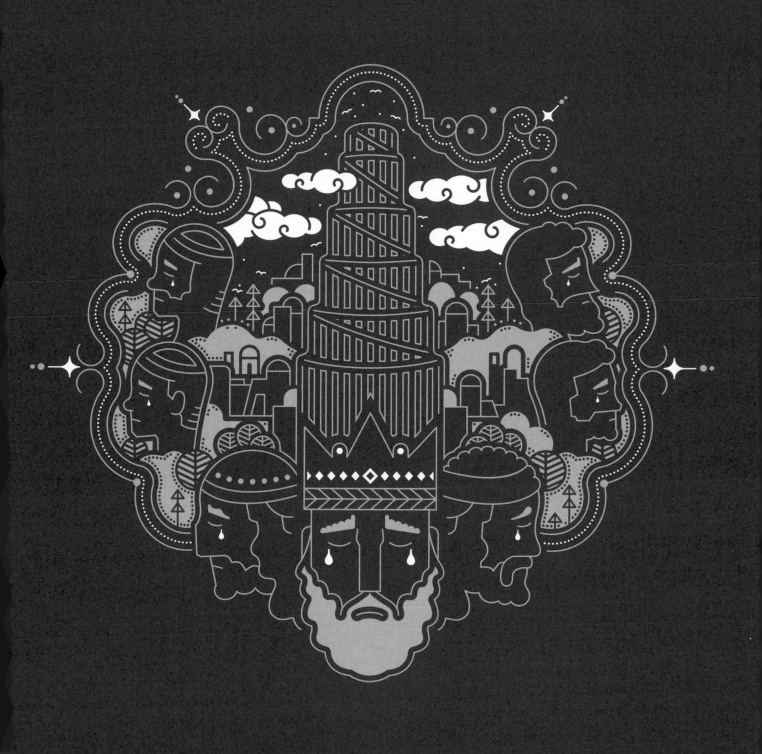

THE RESULTS OF SIN

SIN CHANGES EVERYTHING

But this isn't the only consequence. In fact, sin's poison has seeped into everything in God's once perfect creation.

First, sin breaks the world. Adam's rebellion contaminates all of creation. Sin is why green grass turns brown, crops turn to dust, rivers run dry, and gardens become deserts. With a bite of fruit, Adam's world fell under a curse and, to this day, creation "groans" to be remade (Rom. 8:19–22). Adam's sin cursed the ground, and your sin still puts you at odds with creation. You water the ground with your sweat. You rule creation through pain. The world used to be where we *found* joy, but now, it's what you *fight* against for joy.

Sin, then, is why you always have to pull weeds in the heat of summer, why schoolwork is so difficult and never-ending, and why winters feel so bleak and gray. And here is the dreariest news of all: at the end of your life, the ground wins. Because sin brings death, everyone born after Adam will return to the dust.

And here's the strange thing: Adam's children tend to fall in love with the world's ruins. Many exchange the love meant for their Creator for their misplaced love of creation. Sin twists us up so much that it can make you worship the ground that demands your sweat, is a major source of your pain, and will eventually become your grave.

Second, sin breaks you. As if this weren't bad enough, sin not only corrodes creation, it also corrodes you. From the inside. It eats away at your loves, hopes, and dreams. Sin mixes them all up and puts them back in the wrong place. It twists the way you feel about yourself, others, and, well, everything. What are the first feelings Adam and Eve feel after their rebellion? Fear, shame, and guilt—emotions that were never felt in Eden before the serpent's fork-tongued lies.

Outside of this garden, then, our hearts are still topsy-turvy. Half the time you don't know how to feel, and the rest of the time your feelings are wrong. Even your desires and hopes don't work right. But the problem isn't with your heart wanting things; no, the King made you to desire. The problem is with *what* you long for. Ever since Adam, you desire the wrong things. You've quietly made the world all about *you*.

But the world doesn't work this way. It can't. If *everyone* thinks *everything* centers on him or her, then the world has no real center. The King, though, made the world for something bigger and better than your selfishness. He made everything about him, which means that you and your desires make sense only when the King reigns at the center of your life and heart.

Sin's power is that it blinds you to this true joy. It makes you like the son who tries to take over his parent's bank account after beating them at Monopoly for the first time. The son won the game but missed the point. He's forgotten why the game exists; he's forgotten that his parents bought him the game with *their* real (not Monopoly) money to enjoy time with *their* son. Likewise, sin makes you forget that everything you have, the King gave you so that you might enjoy *him*. Your temptation will always be to desire the King's kingdom while hating the King.

Now, if you want to know if you really struggle with misplaced desires, just ask yourself what you think about most of the day or what you do with your free time. Is it video games? Your phone? What others think about you? Fashion? Maybe it's something else, but often it's something other than your King, isn't it? These things aren't sinful themselves, but when they replace the King, they reveal that *you* are sinful.

Sin infects your heart and your head too. Maybe you've seen this before. Have you ever watched someone use his smarts to come up with a brilliantly bad way to cheat off someone else's homework rather than just use his smarts for

his own work? Or maybe you've used your own brainpower to trick others to do what you want them to do. Perhaps you've used your smarts to try to even outsmart your King, the King who gave you your smarts to begin with.

Sin messes with your head. It turns your good sense inside out and upside down. It's how you know that everyone is a sinner but you never think of *yourself* as one. It's why you see other people's sin so easily but can't see that same sin in your own heart.

Sin doesn't make sense and, because of this, it poisons everything, including your relationship with other sinners. After falling into temptation, Adam and Eve's sin spreads to each other. Eve doesn't want to be Adam's helper and Adam wants to blame Eve for everything. What else would happen when two people poisoned by sin try to relate to one another? Sooner or later, you will hurt those you love and they will hurt you. Sin is why you have to say you are sorry. It's also why your friends don't always seem to be your friends and why it's so hard to say nice things to your family sometimes.

Sin messes up everything—in the world, in you, and in your relationships with other sinners.

Third, sin breaks your relationship with the King. This is sin's biggest nightmare. Ever since the first temptation, God's image bearers have been trying to hide from the very one whose image they bear. After the fruit incident, Adam and Eve ran away from their King, when they should have run *to* him. He was and is the only answer to all the problems their rebellion created—and the problems our rebellion continues to create. People are still hiding from the only one who can rescue them from their sin.

There is a big problem, though. The King in his perfect holiness can't and won't have sin near him. The King will not stand for rebellion. He does not allow rebels in his kingdom.

Something has to be done.

And the King does just that. Where Adam's sin ripped a hole in the world, the King filled it with fitting curses and punishments (and grace—more on that soon). The King warned Adam and Eve from the beginning: if you eat the forbidden fruit, you get death. And so, with Adam's bite, death entered into God's perfect creation. First on the scene was spiritual death, which simply means that Adam and everyone after him stand separated from the love, life, and light of the King. Because of spiritual death, Adam and Eve can't stay in Eden, the special place of the King's presence, and neither can you. Like the first couple, you stand outside of the King's love if you are still in rebellion against him.

Spiritual death leads to physical death. Adam's sin puts life on this earth on a timer. Your life is like a clock running out of time before the alarm. Soon sin's ugly "friend," physical death, will be waiting to take you out of this world. No one can avoid death because no one has avoided sin.

And yet, physical death is not the "end" end. It is like the end of the beginning or the end of the first book in your favorite series of books. Life continues after death. But the life to come is different; it is eternal. This means those who suffer spiritual death now will be separated from the King—the one you were made to delight in, the only one who offers eternal joy and hope—not only in this life, but in the forever life to come.

Sin changes everything, especially your relationship with the King in this world and the next.

THE ANSWER TO SIN

THE KING TURNS YOUR DARKNESS INTO LIGHT

This serpent key unlocks a dark, dark truth about yourself, about your world, and about everyone else. Yet, the King—motivated by his huge love—can turn your darkness into light. For it is against this darkness that his beauty shines in full brilliance. Sin is not the end of your story, or at least it doesn't have to be. While the serpent, sin, and shame shout their demands, God graciously writes a better story by writing his Word into his world. And with overwhelming mercy, the King turns your curses and punishments into the true hope that actually heals you.

You read that right. The King uses the dreadful *curses* you earned to give you his perfect *promises* you don't deserve. He turns sin's power into sin's defeat. While punishing sin in Genesis 3, the King hints at his grace. He promises to send a child—one of Adam and Eve's great, great, great, etc. grandchildren—into his world to "unbreak" his world. This Son will make everything right again by killing the serpent. By being crushed by spiritual and physical death himself, this Promised One will crush the head of the serpent, destroy sin, and conquer death once and for all.

To draw out sin's poison, the King sends his Son to drink the poison, so you don't have to.

Turn the next key and watch what the King does.

Everything goes dark when you turn the key. But it's a different kind of dark, the kind of dark you felt in the void before the world was made. This is the dark you feel right before morning dawns. The kind that seems to be waiting for sunlight to conquer it.

And after a while, the soft light of day finally breaks in, allowing you to see the surroundings you've only been able to smell and touch thus far.

Even with the thin light, you don't know where you are. You can't recognize anything. There is no sky above or grass below. Instead, stone and earth border you on every side, except behind you, where the sun sneaks in. There you see the massive circle of rock that someone or something has somehow rolled away from your chamber's man-carved entryway.

Outside the stone door is a garden choked with weeds and thorns and the familiar sounds of a city starting its hectic and hurried day outside the garden's gates.

But it's not what is outside your stone door that steals your interest; it's what you find inside. Against one of the walls lies a pile of linen cloth strong with the smell of oil and spices.

Then the wise and familiar voice echoes off the stone walls surrounding you . . .

THE PERSON OF CHRIST

CHRIST, THE DEATH KILLER

**Y**our hope hinges on Another. Eden taught you that you need someone to take your poison. Eden taught you that you cannot save yourself. Those drowning in the ocean don't throw themselves life preservers. Those whose hearts stop beating can't make their hearts beat again on their own.

So it is with sin. You can't rescue yourself from your sin, because with sin you aren't just in danger of dying, you're already spiritually dead. Sinners are like prisoners on death row—the King's just and right court has already declared their death sentences. Sinners are just waiting for the verdict to be carried out.

You can try and try and try to make your world right. You can run from your sins and your problems. But no matter how hard you try and no matter how hard you run, they will still be there.

That's why you are standing in a tomb right now. This is where your sin finally catches up with you. A pitch-black grave is where everyone's story ends. The graveyard waits for everyone, including you. And Death always delivers because Death always gets his man, or his woman, or his boy, or his girl. Because Death has a secret: he has power over everyone because everyone is a sinner.

Except for one.

This one. This one whose tomb you stand in right now. He is different. Have you seen it? Have you seen what is different about his tomb?

His tomb is empty; his tomb is open.

That is because he is the Death Killer. This is his promise and his name.

But you may know him by one of his many other names.

Some call him the *Son of God* in order to announce his "divine other-than-ness" and distinction from the world. He calls himself the *Son of Man*, so he could freely define himself through his life, teachings, and work during his life on earth. He also goes by *Lord*, a title reserved for God alone. Others simply know him as the *Christ*, the Messiah, the "one anointed" or "christened" to rescue humanity from sin and death. Others call him by his name, *Jesus*, quietly declaring that "he will save his people from their sins" every time they speak this name (Matt. 1:21).

Now the Death Killer has many other names, but if you stop to combine the truth contained just in these, you have a beautiful mosaic of Christ's full-spectrum beauty and work.

The Death Killer is more than you could ever imagine because you need him to do the unimaginable for you.

BEFORE THE WORLD BEGAN

Just think about how his story starts.

What happens when you think about the Son's beginning? Do visions of shepherds, angels, wise men, and mangers fill your head? If so, you have to think *bigger*. His story is bigger than Christmas. In fact, it's too big to have a start at all. The Death Killer has always been. He didn't begin that night outside an ancient inn in Bethlehem. He didn't even begin before that. No, he was and is and will be eternally with the Father and the Spirit, because he is God. He is the divine Son, one of the "who's" in the three-in-one God; he has always existed because existing is who God is and what God does.

THE DEATH KILLER TAKES ON FLESH

But God doesn't just make the world; he saves it. It's in God's rescue plan that we see the Death Killer's "Son-specific" beauty. You see, the Son doesn't just help put the rescue mission together; the Son actually *is* the rescue mission. He left the comforts of heaven because the Father sent him to invade his creation to help his people out of the grave and back to God.

That is why Christmas is more than wrapping paper and stockings hung by the chimney with care. It is the celebration of the *incarnation*. It is when the incredible became the unfathomable: the "other than" God becomes God "in the flesh" to be "God with us." The divine Son becomes the God-man. The one who always was, is, and will be, was born to a woman because the Holy Spirit mysteriously made it so. The baby sleeping in the manger—the one under the watchful eyes of his virgin mother, Mary, and earthly father, Joseph—created the world he was just born into. The wood for his manger? His. The animals in the field around him? His. The parents who would protect him and provide for him? His.

The Creator did the unthinkable; he became a part of his creation. For sinners like you.

This is why you have to think bigger when you think about the Death Killer. His is a complex beauty. His light glimmers in Bethlehem, shines in Nazareth, appears extinguished on Calvary, but outshines the sun when he steps out of the tomb you stand in now.

The Death Killer is so important and so unique because he is—somehow, at the same time—like you and different from you.

Or to put it another way, Jesus is—at the same time—fully man and fully God.

Jesus is perfectly human. The Word became flesh. He, like you, has a human body. He was born and he grew up. He felt tired like you, was thirsty and hungry like you, he felt weak like you, and he even died like you will one day. He grew in wisdom and knowledge and even has feelings like you. He marveled, he knew sorrow, he was deeply moved, and he was troubled.

Jesus even cried like you when he saw the effects of Adam's curse in his world.

Now this may seem strange. How can this be true when you don't know any other people like Jesus? In a way, the question answers itself. It is true *because* there is no one else like him. To deal with sin and death you need a man who is like you in every way, except he must be perfect. You need to know that Christ is perfectly human; he is like you in every way, *yet without sin*.

In fact, Jesus is more human than you are. He is like Adam, but better. He is sinless and never sins.

This is one of the reasons it's so hard to *know* the Death Killer. You've only known a sin-wrecked world, and you just think the world is supposed to be like this. You think that death is natural, tears are normal, and giving in to temptation is just the way life goes. Like a child who's lived all her life underground would have no idea what to do with the sun, forest, or ocean, sinners have a hard time understanding a sinless Jesus.

That's why—if you really take time to read his book and hear his speech—Jesus's life and teaching are so shocking. It can even make you uncomfortable. His life and words teach us that the world isn't the way it's supposed to be and that he offers you a better path. He offers you his kingdom—the right-side-up world in the middle of our upside-down world. But to sinners' ears, the King and his kingdom sound just the opposite. So the world rejects him, and his enemies seek to silence him.

Many thought they could do this to Jesus. They thought they could make him go away because they thought he was *only* a man. And if he were, then silencing him might have been an option. But the empty tomb you stand in teaches you that the Death Killer is more than just a man. He is *God* with you.

In fact, Jesus's "divine other-than-ness" colors all of his earthly life and work. Like his Father, Jesus knows everything, is everywhere, finds all his life in himself, rules over creation, always existed, and is the Creator of all things. He remains perfectly holy, answers his followers' prayers, performs miracles, fulfills prophecy, forgives sins, receives worship, and—as you see in this empty tomb— defeats death, one of your biggest enemies.

This is his testimony: The Death Killer is the God-man. He is the Son of God and Jesus of Nazareth. He is bigger, more perfect, and more unique than you can even imagine. And yet, like the bustling city streets right outside his tomb, the world passes by day after day, not even giving the most important person this world has ever known a second thought.

THE WORK OF CHRIST

THE DEATH KILLER'S ACTIONS

Do not be like the world.

Do not ignore the Death Killer.

Think hard about who he is. To do this, just remember that if you really want to understand *who* the God-man is, you have to understand *why* God became man in the first place. To know Jesus is to know his mission; to know his mission is to know Jesus. Who Jesus is and what he does are inseparable. So to know him well—for him to be the one who kills death *for you*—think hard about the three important acts that make up his divine drama.

ACT 1: THE DEATH KILLER DIES ON A CROSS

First, why did the Death Killer invade his creation? He tells us himself when he says that "the Son of Man came not to be served but to serve, and to give his life as a ransom for many" (Matt. 20:28).

God became man to trade places with sinners. Sinners deserve death and judgment because of how they've betrayed and double-crossed the King. Yet this is the beauty of the gospel: that same "other than" King you betrayed became the "near you" King to rescue sinners like you from their sin. That means the Death Killer came to die. For his enemies. The sinless one piled up all his people's sins on his back and carried them up the cross. The very rebels he came to save hammered nails into his hands and feet, pushed a thorny crown onto his head, and suspended him between heaven and earth on two wooden beams.

Why did the Son of God allow this to take place? Because Jesus came to defeat sin, death, and the serpent at their own game. He came to make things right again by having the greatest wrong in the history of the world committed against him. The Death Killer came to deal once and for all with sin and death so that his people might have freedom and eternal life. And he did all of this for you by becoming your stand-in.

Imagine your older brother telling your Mom and Dad that he would be glad to be grounded instead of you right after you disrespected and lied to them. It's hard to imagine your brother—or anyone for that matter—ever doing that for you, isn't it? Now imagine the King of the cosmos doing that for all the sins that image bearers—like you—ever committed against him.

It is almost too wonderful and too big and too much. But that is exactly how the King's love always is. God came down to be pierced for your transgression; he came down to be crushed for your iniquities. Your punishment was poured out on him so that his wounds might heal you. When you should be facing the punishment for your sins, he has already taken that punishment himself on the cross.

If he is *your* Death Killer.

All of this is yours, *if* God is your King. If he's not, well then, you face this punishment on your own, for all eternity.

ACT 2: THE DEATH KILLER KILLS DEATH

Now, why did the Death Killer not stay in the grave? Because Christ's resurrection—his being raised to life after death—shows you that God's rescue plan really worked. Without the resurrection, sin and death still control you. They are like a virus that has no earthly cure. Jesus, though, is the God-man who became the antidote for your disease. He swallowed your virus, suffered

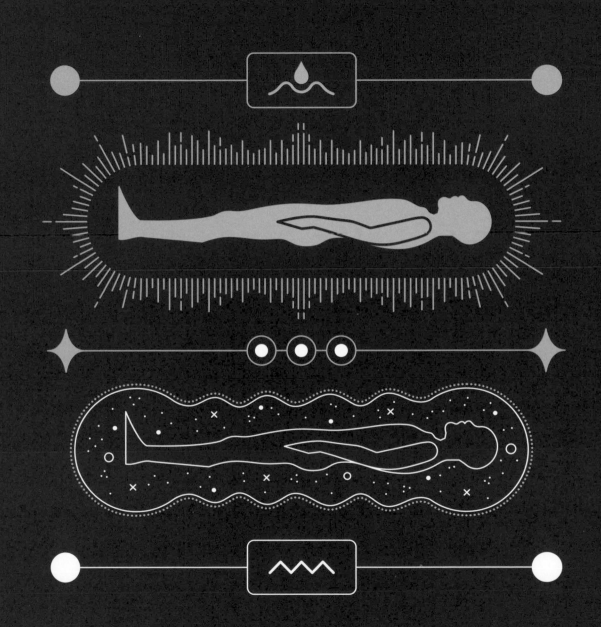

its consequences, and showed the world that your disease has no power over him. That is the picture of the resurrection: Christ takes on your sin, suffered sin's death, and killed death's power with his resurrection. God can be your King because Jesus stepped out of his tomb.

So you must remember that while the Death Killer died for sinners, he was raised from the dead for them too. This is his victory song. The empty tomb shouts that Jesus is your rescuer! It announces that Christ's death really did make a way out of the grave and into eternal life with the King. Because sin could not hold him, death had no power over him.

In the resurrection, God's right-side-up kingdom begins to fix the upside-down world we currently know and live in. The power of God's saving death is fueled by the power of Christ's resurrected life. The empty tomb is the open doorway to the very real, very eternal, better-than-this-world life. Christ's being risen from the dead means the King has finally and fully taken away Death's sting for those who belong to his kingdom.

Do you remember?

Your hope hinges on Another.

That hope blossomed with every step Jesus took outside of this tomb. And that hope continues to spread through those who have made his resurrection their own.

ACT 3: THE DEATH KILLER TAKES HIS RIGHTFUL PLACE

I know what you are thinking. You want to know where the Death Killer is now, don't you? The answer to that lies in two "returns."

First, the Son returned, or ascended, to the Father. After forty days of ministry and teaching, the resurrected Jesus took his rightful place at the right hand of his Father. Christ's earthly work connects heaven and earth. The one who suffered on earth now has all rule, power, authority, and dominion forever given to him in heaven. This is why the Death Killer's return to the heavenly throne room doesn't mean his earthly work is done. No, he continues to work for those he came to rescue.

Notice what his return to heaven means. Christ brought humanity into the heavenly places. Don't miss this. Christ didn't stop being human in the resurrection and the ascension; instead, he made humanity right and demonstrated that you, an image bearer, are welcome before the King. That is, if you belong to the Death Killer.

This leads to another work in his ascension. The Death Killer now stands before the Father, pleading your case based on the merits of his own death and resurrection. If you are his, he stands up against any blame the world or the serpent throws at you. If you are his, the Death Killer is praying for you before his Father's throne.

But he never promised to remain in heaven. This is why there is a second return, or what those in your world call the second coming. The Death Killer pledges to come back to earth again to complete all of his promises. Even though Christ defeated sin and death, you still face a world filled with sin and death, don't you? This is not because his work didn't work but because it's actually a gift. The time between his ascension and his second coming allows rebels time to return to their rightful King.

In his return to earth, the Death Killer will deal with sin, death, and the serpent once and for all. He will finally punish all his enemies—including every man, woman, boy, and girl who rejected him as the true King. This is how he makes all things right. His second coming puts everything back into its proper orbit, wrings the sadness out of the world, unites heaven with earth, and places the King's throne at the center of this world made new.

This promise—like a hemline—pulls the threads of Christ's earlier cross, resurrection, and ascension work together with the hope of Christ's future work. This one—this Lord, Son of God, Son of Man, this Christ Jesus, this Death Killer— brings eternity past together with eternity future. He brings God to man, man to God, Christmas to Easter, the beginning to the end, and—if he is your King—he unites you to himself.

The question remains, Where do you place your hope? Does it rest in the Death Killer making a way back to the King?

There is only one way to find out.

Turn the key, to see what the Death Killer has done for you.

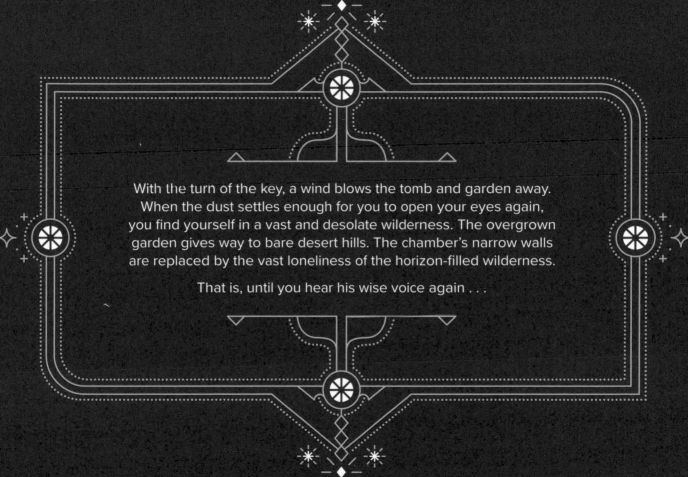

With the turn of the key, a wind blows the tomb and garden away.
When the dust settles enough for you to open your eyes again,
you find yourself in a vast and desolate wilderness. The overgrown
garden gives way to bare desert hills. The chamber's narrow walls
are replaced by the vast loneliness of the horizon-filled wilderness.

That is, until you hear his wise voice again . . .

THE SPIRIT LIVES

YOUR GREATEST NEED IS A NEW HEART

our greatest need is a new heart.

That is why the Spirit led the Son here into the wilderness. What seems like the last place for a King's Son was the very place the King needed him to be. What the world didn't know, the Holy Spirit did, which is why the Spirit brought him into the desert. He brought the Death Killer—the better image of God, the Son of Man—to do what Adam didn't do, what you could not do.

The Spirit brought the Death Killer into the wilderness to face the serpent's cruel test and to overthrow his temptations with the Spirit's own words. The beginning of the end starts here. In the desert, the Death Killer places his heel over the ancient serpent's head and then waits for the perfect time to deal the death blow.

The Spirit does all of this because the Spirit was faithful to lead the Son into the Father's deep, never-forgotten promises.

This is what the Spirit does. He makes everything about the Son. He even made this wilderness story about the King's Son, which, of course it is. But even when you want to look at his work, the Spirit somehow always makes it about the Death Killer.

That's his ministry, though. That is the way he works—and it is beautiful.

Still, the Spirit deserves his rightful due—not because he seeks it but because he is God himself. To know God and his rescue plan, you have to know the Spirit too. He is the one to turn the Death Killer's work into an antidote for your dead heart. He makes your heart alive again. Here is the Spirit's brilliance: he's always there but he never takes center stage—he leaves that for the Son. Though you may have to look a little harder for him from time to time, it's always worth the look.

You first must know who the Spirit is—or perhaps, what the Spirit is not. To be sure, the Spirit is not just some sort of mysterious force or a fleeting feeling. He is not some thing or some stuff. He is a "he" not an "it." Oh no, the Holy Spirit is God—the Trinitarian God of the Bible. He is the third person of the Trinity. He is one of the "who's" that shares the same "what." He is equal with the Father and the Son because he shares the same essence as the Father and the Son.

This Spirit also acts like a person would act. Take note of what God's speech tells us about him. Like the people you know, the Spirit also thinks, chooses, and acts freely, though he does all of these things perfectly because he is divine. He also feels emotions and experiences things in similar ways that people do. But you really know that the Spirit is a person because you can have a personal relationship with him just like you can with the Father and the Son.

THE SPIRIT WORKS

THE DIVINE ACTIONS OF THE HOLY SPIRIT

nowing who the Spirit is helps makes sense of what the Spirit does. Who the Spirit is and what the Spirit does are both about God's glory and your good. In the Spirit, God is working out his own promises for his people by the Spirit living in his people. The Spirit is the quiet one who slowly and steadily waters all of the King's plans and promises so they finally take root and blossom into your hope and happiness.

THE SPIRIT CREATES

That is why the Holy Spirit is there from the very beginning. Think about where you stand right now. How did the Death Killer get here to the wilderness? The Spirit led him here, and he did so to ensure God's pledge to save his world and people. But the Spirit was working out God's promises long before Jesus's feet got dusty. In fact, the Spirit was a part of creation's "grand opening." He was with the Father and the Son, creating order out of chaos and bringing light out of darkness. He hovered over the waters, and he was there deciding and declaring who the King's image bearers were supposed to be.

THE SPIRIT RESCUES

Rescuing sinners is also the Spirit's goal. Before Jesus's incarnation, the Spirit helped the world look for God's Promised One—the one the King would send to save rebels like you. The Spirit helped prepare the way for Jesus's work on the earth by anointing prophets to speak (and write) God's speech down. He worked through Israel's priests to help them stand between the holy King and his disobedient people. He also worked to guide and inspire the artists and craftsmen chosen by God to build and beautify the tabernacle and temple. The Spirit's early work focused on guiding the nation's leaders—especially the judges and kings—toward the good things God had for them.

The Holy Spirit's "before the incarnation" ministry sheds light on his "during the incarnation" ministry. He was always at work, and when the Son came, the Spirit was like an orchestra's conductor slowly increasing the tempo of his masterpiece. Jesus is the Spirit's crescendo! The Spirit's central desire when you turn the page from the book of Malachi to the book of Matthew is to help people see that Jesus is the one the King promised long ago.

The Spirit wants you to see that everything he did before the incarnation led to the incarnation. The Spirit rested upon Israel's prophets, priests, and kings in order to prepare the way for Jesus to be the better Prophet, Priest, and King.

How do you know that Jesus is the better prophet—the better Moses? How do you know that Jesus is a better priest—the one who stands between God and you? How is he also the once-and-for-all sacrifice for sins? How do you know that Jesus is the better King who begins the right-side-up kingdom in this upside-down world? The one who is like David and yet far surpasses him in everything? You know this because of the Spirit. He's like the headlights on your car. You never look directly into the headlights because that is not the purpose of the headlights. They are there to show you what is up ahead. The Spirit's ministry to the Son is the same way. He shines his light on the Death Killer because he wants your eyes on the one who comes before you to rescue you.

Here's the beautiful thing: From the beginning of his story, God promised that he would pour out his Spirit on *all* of his people. The Son himself promised that when his work on the cross was finished, the Spirit would come to guide, help, teach, and dwell *inside* believers. That is why soon after the Son ascended to his Father after his resurrection, the Spirit descended upon Jesus's followers. He came to dwell inside them and spread the King's kingdom to the rest of

the world by ministering through them. The Spirit is the divine and personal machine that the Father and the Son send into the world to build Christ's church, complete God's promises, apply the Son's work to former rebels, and guarantee that the King's people don't stop being his people.

On this side of Jesus's empty tomb, the Spirit helps lead this chapter of God's rescue plan. First he gives us God's playbook, the Bible. The Holy Spirit ensured, established, and directed the writing of Scripture. Sure, Scripture has human authors. You've probably heard of Paul and John, maybe even Isaiah and Moses. But don't forget that there is a divine author too. He is the Spirit—once again in the background—working in and through gifted yet flawed men to ensure a rich, beautiful, personal, and simultaneously perfect Bible. Through the Spirit, God interprets himself for you. The stories, letters, poems, and proverbs of the Bible aren't just man's thoughts about God; they are God's thoughts about himself through the hearts and minds of men filled with and directed by the Holy Spirit.

It's like when a river flows through a lake. While there are two bodies of water for a time, they become one, with the river moving through and in the lake to reach its destination. The Spirit moves through and works within the human authors to produce a Bible with a divine and human authorship about a divine and human God who comes to bring humans back to the divine.

But remember how the Spirit works. He's in the front row pointing toward Jesus who stands on the world's center stage. It's the same with his book. The Spirit makes sure that Jesus is the hero of his masterpiece from start to finish. Every letter, word, and paragraph is a beam of light in the spotlight of the Son's triumphant victory.

One of the Spirit's greatest works is turning the King's enemies into the King's followers. The Spirit takes Christ's accomplishments and gives them to God's people. The Spirit who created the world also re-creates the world and God's people. The same Spirit who brought a baby from a virgin and led Christ from a manger to the resurrection is the Spirit who can apply God's rescue plan to you. All of God's work and promises become yours through the Spirit. He readies the world for the King's rescue. He shows you that you are a sinner who cannot save yourself. But the Spirit also makes the good news of Christ's rescue mission good news *for you*, making Christ's work yours and making you new again.

The Spirit, though, doesn't just leave you there. He keeps working. He indwells believers, he baptizes believers, and he fills believers. The Spirit connects God's people with Jesus and his benefits. That is why he is called the "Spirit of adoption." He takes those outside of God's family and makes them a part of God's family. He helps those who once called God their enemy to now call him "Abba, Father."

THE SPIRIT ACHIEVES

This Spirit remains with his people. He continues to live in them until he finishes the King's work in you. The Spirit is with his people for the long haul. His work isn't a once-in-a-lifetime deal; it's a for-a-lifetime-and-into-eternity deal. So not only does the Spirit rescue sinners, he also makes sure they stay rescued. He places you in Christ's kingdom and gives you gifts to help build and expand Christ's kingdom. And while he calls you to be holy like Jesus, he actually helps you to do that. He works in you to make sure that, over time, you hate sin more and love the world less than you used to.

If you are his, then, you will carry his mark. The Spirit presses his seal upon you. The Spirit's seal tells you and the world that you belong to the King forever and that the King's promises belong to you forever too. And how do you know this? Because the Spirit is the seal and the seal is the Spirit.

The Spirit who does all of this can live *within you*. He is the one who can unite you to the Death Killer. The Spirit is the one who opens the doors to the King's kingdom and the one who can keep you there.

Are you brave enough to walk through those doors? Do you want to know what lies on the other side? If you are, turn the key to see just what the Spirit offers you.

Turning the key causes a great wind to blow out of the East that drives all the sand, rocks, and hills away. A calm sets in. Starlight, breaking through the night sky overhead, dimly shines on a narrow path that leads to an even narrower gate. Passing through it, you find a sea of crystal-clear glass on the other side, and on the far shoreline sits a majestic, emerald-colored throne surrounded by twenty-four smaller thrones. As you strain to see the beautiful sight across the sea, something catches your eye. On the center throne sits what seems to be a large book or scroll of some kind. Seeing it floods you with dread and hope at the same time. You cringe, weep, and laugh simultaneously. Somehow, you know this book is unlike any other book. It reads you, not the other way around.

But there is a reason a sea separates you from the throne and the book. No matter how much you want to read its words, you know you can never open its pages. Tears overcome you as you feel the weight of your unworthiness. And while everything you've always wanted lies on the throne across the sea, it might as well be ten thousand miles away.

But that's when you hear it coming from the far shore. Something strange. Something odd. Like the mixture of a lion's roar and a sheep's bleat. But that doesn't do the sound justice— it's more beautiful than that. Hearing it fills you with your favorite feelings. It comforts your soul—like hot chocolate in a snowstorm—and floods your heart with eager anticipation—like sunrise on Christmas morning. And then the sound stops.

You would be happy to hear that beautiful, mysterious sound forever. You want nothing more than to hear that lion and lamb speak again. But all you hear now is silence, until that wise, familiar voice whispers to you once again . . .

THE WATERS OF SALVATION

YOUR RANSOM CAN BE PAID

our ransom can be paid.

Take a step if you want to meet the one who can open the book and show it to you.

Your desire to hear the lion and lamb overcomes your fears. So you close your eyes, take a deep breath, and take a step. Instead of falling into the sea like you expected, the waters come together to form an image of a hand.

THE HAND OF ELECTION

You now stand upon the most secure location ever to exist: the divine Hand of Election. Here are all of the King's purposes in salvation that existed well before the beginning of creation and were designed perfectly by the perfect Trinity. Election is the King's solid, sure, unbreakable plan to save a people for himself for his glory and for their joy. Before he laid the foundations of the world, the King laid out his mission to rescue that very same world.

To see the love that overflows out of the King's hand, just take another step.

And though you don't want to leave the comfort of the King's grip, you want to know more. So you do take another step, and when you do, the water turns to blood and pools together in the wooden form of a weathered and bloodstained *T*.

THE CROSS OF ATONEMENT

Before you stands the instrument of your rescue. This is the Cross of Atonement. You saw this before, when you stood in the empty tomb. You see, the hand of God that holds the King's design for the world is the same hand that directs all of history toward its most important moment: Jesus dying on the cross. Do you

remember why Jesus came? It was to give his life as a ransom for many. He sacrificed himself in order to buy his people back from their slavery to sin. His death breaks the bars of sin and death's prison, while his resurrection frees us from the tomb to enjoy eternal life.

You stand under the cross now because everything you are about to see flows out of Jesus's pierced side. He can buy you back by his death. So if you want to know exactly what the Death Killer's work has done for you, then keep going. Take the next step.

As you do, the water violently rises out of the sea to take the form of a mountain. Strangely, just off the cliff is a wooden door floating in midair.

THE MOUNTAIN OF THE GOSPEL CALL

You now stand atop the Mountain of the Gospel Call. From here, you hear God's story. You hear him tell you about the Death Killer, his cross, and the empty tomb he used to kill death. And you also hear that the Death Killer offers to kill sin and death for you. This is the gospel call. God doesn't only want you to know what he did; he wants you to believe. The King wants you to see that the Death Killer came on behalf of sinners like you. He wants you to hear his promises so that you reject your past life of sin and rebellion. Through the gospel call, the King summons his people to the Door of Conversion.

Do you hear the call? Do you hear his plan of rescue? This is the way to the lion and lamb.

Step off the peak to get closer to the throne and the book.

With the next step, the mountain of water erupts, transforming into what appears to be a man's heart. Except for one thing: the heart appears to be more like stone than human flesh. It is as hard as a rock and motionless as one too. But then there is a change. The upper left chamber begins to beat vigorously, and the color, look, and feel of a real beating heart begins to spread throughout its once rocky exterior. The heart is coming alive.

THE HEART OF REGENERATION

What you see before you is the Heart of Regeneration. This is the power of the gospel: like this heart, the Spirit takes what is dead and makes it alive. He replaces our old, fight-against-the-King hatred with a new, do-anything-for-the-King love. He brings spiritual life to those who are spiritually dead. And everyone is spiritually dead until the Spirit makes them spiritually alive. This is why God speaks so much about new birth and being born again. The Spirit brings you back to spiritual life. He makes your dead eyes alive so that you can finally see that sin is poison and the Death Killer is the only real antidote. Only those who have a Spirit-made heart can reach and open the Door of Conversion.

Now if you want to see more of his beauty, step forward once again.

When you do, the water rises and falls until you stand on the edge of what seems to be an odd-looking hammer.

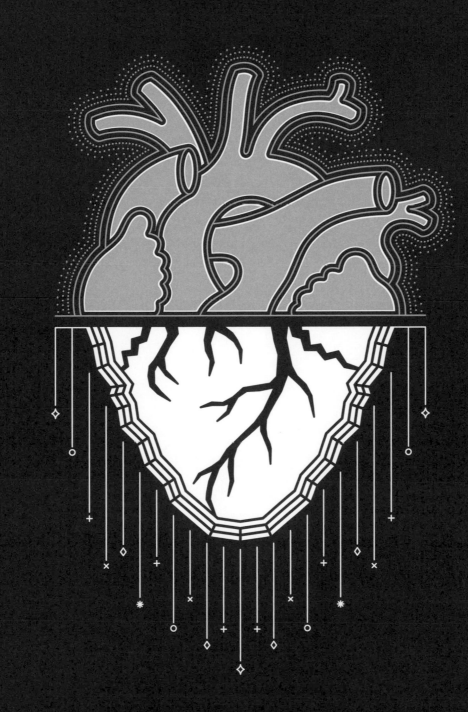

THE GAVEL OF JUSTIFICATION

You stand on the High Judge's Gavel of Justification. If you have a new heart, you have a new hope. You no longer stand under God's just judgment; you stand free. You no longer stand on the enemy's side of the battlefield. You stand on his side, with the righteous Warrior King who will deal once and for all with the lawless rebels.

God does this by declaration. Like a judge, he announces before all hearers that sinners who place their faith in him are no longer guilty; they are righteous before his holy and pure eyes. How is this so? How can lifetime rebels become full-time saints? Because the "other than" King is powerful enough to credit—what your world's theologians call *impute*—the Death Killer's righteousness and holiness to his faith-filled ones. Based on Christ's work, you can trade your sins for his righteousness. Notice how steep the price he paid for your justification, though. God doesn't just sweep his hatred of sin and wrath against sinners under the cosmic rug of the universe. No, for the faith-filled, he pours it out on his Son. The justification of sinners cost the King his Son.

But, as you know, death could not hold him. That is why he is the Death Killer and why he did what he did. The Death Killer died to take your sins to the grave and to die your death in your place so that you might receive the gift of his righteousness and his never-ending rewards.

If you recognize what the King's holiness demands and just how deep his love for you is, step off the gavel.

With your head hung low and a lump in your throat, you take another step. Almost instantly, you find yourself at the entry of a narrow bridge.

THE BRIDGE OF RECONCILIATION

You now stand on the Bridge of Reconciliation. The High King is its architect. He made it so that faith-filled travelers might find their way into his kingdom. Swirling below the bridge are the dark waters of hostility and anger that have existed between God and man ever since the first bite of Eden's forbidden fruit. The King's grace and mercy turned traitors against the kingdom back into citizens of the kingdom. The King restores peace. He turns enemies into friends, letting them cross back into his beautiful country, and giving them a seat at his banquet table.

But he goes even further to restore sinners. Take a step off the bridge to see what else he's done. When you take the next step, the bridge transforms into an oak tree so large that its limbs seem to touch both shores.

THE TREE OF ADOPTION

This is the divine Tree of Adoption. If you belong to the King, then one of these branches is yours. When you follow him in faith, he brings you into his family. He adopts you as his own, giving you your own limb in his family tree. Not only does he take away the bad things that kept you from him, the King also gives you all the good things of being a part of his family. Those who were alienated and separated from him can now run into his arms as his most loved children. Because of the Death Killer's work on the cross, the faith-filled can be a part of the "other than" King's family forever. He can make you a son or daughter of the King. Both the King and the kingdom can be yours. As if that weren't enough, your adoption also gives you a family of brothers and sisters who, just like you, are happy and free in the King's kind grace.

Take the next step to see how all of these brilliant gifts work together.

As you take your next stride, the tree overflows and resettles into a large chain set with indestructible links.

THE CHAIN OF UNION

Before you is the Chain of Union. It binds God's people together with everything you've seen here before the eternal throne. It unites the faith-filled ones with the one they've placed their faith in. It means that the new citizens of the kingdom take on their King's identity. The Death Killer's death, burial, resurrection, and ascension can be yours now. You become one with the one who saves you. That is how you benefit from his death and resurrection. In union with Christ, his death can be your death and his resurrection can be your resurrection. When the world looks at you, they see your Savior.

Remember, too, that this wasn't your idea. You didn't even know how much you need this. Instead, the King came to save those who hated him. He made a way for him to live in you and for you to live in him. And because of that, everything is different. If you are faith-filled, then you've traded the life you once lived in the dark for a life reflecting the beautiful light of the Son. You are like a ray of the sun shining the warm brilliance of your source into the world. You are somehow different and yet indistinguishable—just like Christ and his people.

As beautiful as all of this is, more beauty awaits. If you want to see it, take the next step.

And with that step the chain falls back into the water, and as you fall with it, the water re-forms in just enough time for you to land at the bottom of a flight of stairs.

THE STAIRS OF SANCTIFICATION

These are the Stairs of Sanctification. You see that the King's work of salvation is not a one-time gift. It is an all-the-time-every-day gift. He doesn't leave you after he's accomplished everything you've seen so far. No, you still need to get to his throne and the scroll. Only he can get you there; but that doesn't mean you have nothing to do. The King wants you to climb the stairs. Go ahead and try.

So you try, but you can't move—it's too difficult. It feels like you're stuck in quicksand.

You can't climb on your own because none of this is your work. You need the power of the Holy Spirit. With him dwelling in you, you can walk these stairs. Sanctification is the joint work of the Spirit and the Christian to make the Christian more like the Death Killer over time. If you belong to Jesus, you are going to do everything in your power to become like Jesus. You are going to read about him, pray to him, kill sin that keeps you from him, and try to follow him wherever he takes you. At the same time, the Spirit is working in you to help you want to do all these things and to help you keep doing them. He is there to convict you of sin and empower you to follow your Rescuer. So climb, but climb in the power of the Spirit, for this is the only way to reach the throne on the shore.

Now look up. What do you see way up there at the top of the stairs?

On the last step sits a golden crown.

THE CROWN OF GLORIFICATION

Above you is the Crown of Glorification. It awaits all climbers at the end of their climb. The King makes one for each of his followers. They reflect all the true, good, and beautiful things his citizens have done as his ambassadors. Yet, even the most elegant and regal crown cannot compare to the King's crown. This is why, when you get closer to the throne, you will see that his people are more excited about the King than what lies ahead for them. That is why there is a pile of crowns lying in front of the center throne. His people's greatest delight is to throw their crowns before their true King. Ambassadors can see their King for who he really is—the only one truly worthy of glory.

Think of yourself. What will you want to do when you come face-to-face with the lion who is the lamb? When you meet the one who sings the song of your heart? The only one who can open the scroll for you and for the world?

And with a rush of wind and a wave of water, the stairs are gone and you find yourself back on the far side of the sea. Your heart sinks because everything you've seen seems to be lost to the crystal waters in front of you.

Do you want to hear the worthy one again? Do you want everything you've just seen? Do you want to see the lion and the lamb make everything right?

Well, turn the key and open the lock.

With the turn of your key, the stars above begin to fuse their light together until it becomes so violently bright you have to cover your eyes. When you're finally able to look up again, you find that the throne and sea have been replaced by a humble room with stucco-like walls and simple openings to let in the cool air. The dust-flecked sunlight flooding the room leads your eyes to a large table where, at its center, sit a small plate of bread and a simple cup of wine.

You've heard about this place before but you can't remember what it is. As you stand in the shadows, wracking your brain, trying to place it, you hear his wise voice again . . .

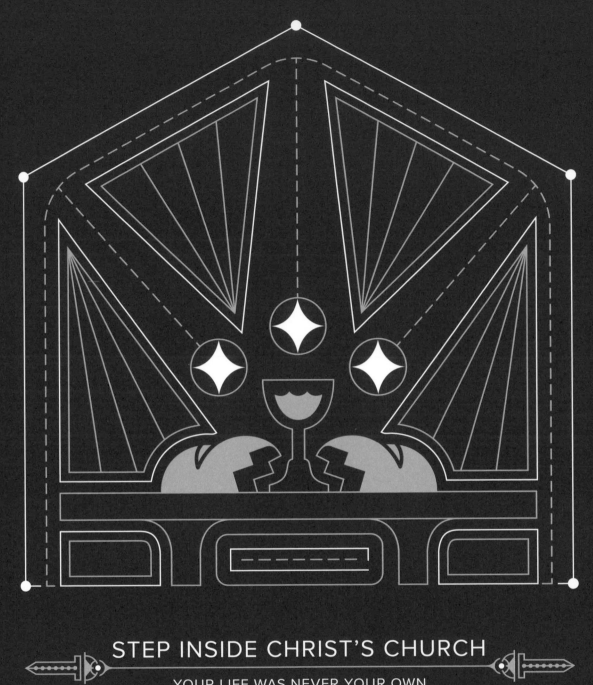

STEP INSIDE CHRIST'S CHURCH

YOUR LIFE WAS NEVER YOUR OWN

From the beginning, your King made you to know, love, and serve others. He made others to do the same for you. That is why—even when they don't recognize it—the people of this world need to create communities, neighborhoods, and towns. It's why humans constantly want to connect with each other. It's why you like the TV on when no one else is around, and it's why your parents are looking at their phones so much. It's why you hope your friend from class invites you to his birthday party.

Your King made you to know and love him and to know and love others like you.

This is why you are in the upper room right now. You see, the King made you this way not only for your happiness but also for your holiness. This is why the Death Killer gathered twelve imperfect men to follow him and why he brought them to this table the night before his death. The bread and wine before you were the beginnings of a new meal he created through his new promises for his new family. It was here that Christ set the course for his own new community, what people in your world call *the church*.

Now there are two ways to think about the church. The first is the local church. This is probably what you think of when you hear that word. The local church is like the one you see on the corner of the street on your way to school. But the local church isn't just that building; it's the people meeting with each other that makes up the church. It is a gathering of faith-filled people who meet together often in a set-aside place to worship the Lord together.

But the Bible talks about a bigger church too—one your world calls *the universal church*. This is the true church without the limits of time or space. That just means that the universal church includes all Christians—anyone and everyone who clings to the Death Killer for their hope and happiness—regardless of age and place. The universal church's membership roll is kept on the lion-lamb's scroll that you saw by the crystal-clear sea. The universal church includes those who live on the other side of the world and even those who no longer live in this world.

The local church and the universal church overlap, but they aren't the same thing. There are those in the universal church who are in the local church, but some in the local church don't have membership in the universal church. Just like your own heart, only the King who made you can perfectly see the universal church he is making. That is why the membership scroll belongs to him and only the Death Killer can open it.

THE IMAGES OF CHRIST'S CHURCH

The King made the church for you. It is his gift to you. So while the world wants you to see it as a duty or a chore or a place filled with boredom, the King wants to open your eyes to its beauty. That is why he fills his Word with word pictures about his church. He wants you to fall in love with the church as the King's Son has fallen in love with her. For as the Word's pictures reveal, the church is the Death Killer's *bride* and he is her Bridegroom. Christ gave his life for the church; he chose her and sacrificially loved her, to the point of death on a cross. The church responds in love and faithfulness to the Bridegroom, remaining loyal to him in a tempting and disloyal world.

The King says that the church is also a *temple*. That is because God is present in the Spirit in the church to change the world. Just as the ancient temple was to be holy, different, set apart, and made for God, so too is Christ's church. God builds the church by his Spirit on the work of Christ so that the Spirit can make all of God's promises yours. The Spirit is with the King's citizens to deliver them into the perfect experience of those promises waiting for you in the future. This is what the temple was for: letting God dwell among his people to make them his own and to get them where he wanted them to be. This is also why the church is God's new temple and why the church must be holy and different from the world.

The church is also the *body* of Christ, and Christ is the head of this church. Think of it this way. Your hand listens to your head when your head tells your hand to turn the key, right? And how do your legs know to run when you see the neighbor's dog get off his leash? Your head tells them too, right? The church works the same way—Christ is the leader of the church; he directs his people in love and wisdom and gives his people his Spirit. He leads them to good things and a happy future. He is the source of her salvation, he gives her his righteousness, and he provides her with his inheritance.

The church then "embodies" Christ to the world that desperately needs to see him. The church is supposed to be his hands and feet in this right here, right now world. As the body works together for one purpose, the members of the body use their Spirit-given gifts to glorify their King and bring the church to wisdom and maturity. That's why his people's character and actions should reflect his character and actions. The church is like the Spirit-made mirror that reflects the King to a world looking for answers in all the wrong places.

The church is God's *family* too. That means that the King is the church's Father, and the King's faith-filled followers are his sons and daughters. This is a ragtag family made up of all kinds of people with all kinds of pasts and all kinds of circumstances. When we see the church as a whole, it looks like a patchwork quilt, with different shapes, patterns, colors, and designs all sewn together by the threads of faith and the King's steady hand. This family exists only because of the King's faithful love expressed in the work of his Son. Christ shed his blood so he could adopt those outside his family to be a people of his own possession. He turned rebels into family members—not because he needed to, but because his glory made a way for you to be his. That is why the church is one of God's biggest miracles.

THE MARKS OF CHRIST'S CHURCH

After some time, the early church began to think long and hard about what it was and what it was supposed to do. As they thought about Scripture and prayed to the King, the Spirit kept bringing four important ideas into their minds, hearts, and conversations. These four ideas soon became known as the four marks or attributes of the church. They were so important, the early church wrote them down so that all of the King's citizens could spot the King's church in the wild, wild world.

The church's first mark is her *oneness*, or unity. This means that Jesus has one church. While the church is already united, it awaits a perfect unity when the King makes everything right in the world. Until then, the one church should strive to live out that unity right here, right now because the kingdom citizens have the same Spirit and share in his truth, love, and mission.

The church should also be *holy*. This second mark means that Christ's work worked: he removed sin's blemish from his people and set her on mission to bring holiness to the world and to one another. The church exists to reflect God's perfection to the world, to declare that God is making a holy people, and to bring his work of holiness to completion. So while the King has made the church holy, he also uses the church to keep the church holy.

The church should also be *catholic* (that's little *c* catholic). Now, the third mark doesn't mean that the Roman Catholic Church (capital *C*) is the only real church in the world; instead, it means that the church is global—it follows the King into all the world. No fences are big enough and no army is strong enough to keep the church out or away from any of his image bearers. The Death Killer's charge to make his name known and to turn enemies into citizens leads to the growth and spread of the church. That's why the sun never sets on Christ's kingdom.

The King made the church to be a worldwide church, shining God's light into every dark corner of the world.

This leads to the last mark of God's people. The church is one, holy, catholic (little *c*), and *apostolic*. This characteristic answers the question, What does the church say to accomplish God's mission? In one word: Scripture—all of it from the Old Testament to the New Testament, from the book of Genesis to the book of Revelation. The church speaks the King's Word to the King's people in the King's world for the King's glory and the King's mission. The King builds his church on the words written by his Son's Spirit-led and faith-filled followers—men known as the Death Killer's apostles. These men walked with the Death Killer during his time on earth and carried his message out into the world upon his ascension. Their words can still be read today in the pages of your Bible. Their words—led by the Spirit and centered on the Son—are the voice of the true church. So as the church finds its life and breath in all of God's Words in all of the Bible, the church lives and breathes because the apostles proclaimed all of these Words to all the world. This is why the good news of Christ forms the center of the church—because the good news of Christ is what all of Scripture is pointing us to.

Where you find these marks, you will find the church of the King. He wants you to know them like a child knows his mother's voice, scent, kiss, and face by heart—because these marks are reflections of the King's ways and the King's kingdom breaking into this world.

THE ACTS OF CHRIST'S CHURCH

To know the church well also means that you know what she does and why she gathers.

The church exists for worship. The faith-filled gather with one another to set their eyes on the King. They assemble to turn their ears to his Word. The church meets to have her hearts fall deeper in love with the King because the King first loved her and bought her with his Son's blood. This is why the church sings, reads, hears, and preaches the King's speech back to him. Not because he needs it (though he does delight in it) but because you do, and through it he tells you how to find your way back to him, now and forever.

While Word and worship are vital to the church's life, this is not all she does. In fact, the church has two unique habits that make her different from everything else. These are what those in your world call *sacraments* or *ordinances*. You may know them by other names. They are *baptism* and the *Lord's Supper*. These are foundational for the church because these sacraments have everything to do with what the Death Killer did for his church.

Take the sacrament of baptism, for example. Baptism is the God-designed megaphone the church uses to announce to the world that the faith-filled's loyalty lies with the King. It pictures for all who are watching what your King has already done for his followers personally. It shows the outside world the good and glorious work God already did on the inside. That is why this sacrament is the first thing you do after you confess your faith in the Death Killer and repent of your sins against him.

Baptism is the gospel put on visible display. Here is how. When the Death Killer's followers go under the water, they announce, through a real-life picture, that

they share in the Death Killer's death. When the Death Killer's followers come up from the water, they announce, in that same real-life picture, that they share in the Death Killer's new life. Baptism shows the world that the Death Killer killed your death with his death and that the Death Killer's resurrected life is your life now. Baptism is all about your unity with Christ. Through pictures and images, it shows you how you can be a part of his body—that what he did on the cross and in the empty tomb, he did for you.

That is why baptism is not only God's megaphone; it is also the handle on the church's front door. While baptism shows the world who you belong to, it also tells the church that you are under her care and now an active member of her body and a part of her life.

The second sacrament sits in front of you right now. This is the Lord's Supper. This meal defines Christ's church. The bread before you pictures Christ's body which—when the bread is torn into pieces—is broken for his followers. The wine before you mirrors Jesus's blood that—when he pours it out—he has shed for his people.

This meal—rich with gospel beauty that stirs the imagination—belongs to the church because only those who are his can take their Savior in like this. The Death Killer made the Lord's Supper for all who belong in the King's kingdom. It is their privilege to eat at their Lord's Table, and it is the first course of the promised never-ending banquet that awaits the church in a remade world. For now, the Lord's Supper is one of the ways the Lord helps the church keep her tired eyes focused on his Son's life-giving and soul-keeping love. When you see it, you see the Death Killer's drama played out in the beautiful symbols the King designed, and when you partake of the divine meal, you know and experience God's good gifts spiritually.

For the church to be a church, she cannot and must not neglect these sacraments. Both belong to the church to help God's people know, remember, hear, taste, feel, and see what Christ has done for her. The King uses them to picture how the gospel affects every part of who you are, down to every one of your senses. They define the church and mark his people out as his own.

THE MISSION OF CHRIST'S CHURCH

As you heard in the desert, the Spirit guides his people, which means the church is going somewhere. The church is on a mission. Even though the building doesn't move, the people in the building are to be moving forward into the world for the King.

You see, the Spirit wants to make his church more like her Savior. He also wants to use his church to do so. The Spirit will get his people to the end of God's story, and the church is one of the main ways he will do this. Remember, your life is never your own. The Spirit uses the people in the church, with all their wisdom and all their problems, to shape you and prepare you for the new creation. The church is just what God planned to use to make you more like Christ.

This puts the church in the right place. It doesn't exist to glorify you; it exists to help you become more like the Death Killer. The church is an instrument in the Spirit's hands. He uses all the people who act and think differently than you not to annoy you, but to help you grow in godliness. And you and all your quirks—by the Spirit's direction—help them grow too.

But the church's mission doesn't just take place within its own walls—it goes out into all the world too. Every time you step outside the church, you are back among the rebels. You aren't there to fear them or to run from them or to judge them.

You are there to tell them the good news about the Death Killer, so they can enter into his kingdom, partake of his life-giving death, and rejoice in the one they currently hate. The church's mission is not only to keep the faith-filled on the narrow path to God's future gifts, it's also called by God to help the faithless become filled with faith too.

The question remains, do you belong to Christ's church? Are you marching with the church on the narrow path toward his too-good-to-be-true-but-really-are promises?

If you want to catch a glimpse of the promises that await the King's citizens, then turn the final key. But before you do, be warned: you cannot unsee what lies on the other side of this lock.

And so you close your eyes and, with a deep breath, you turn the last key one last time.

8
THE THRONE KEY

THE DOCTRINE OF LAST THINGS

Your lungs sting as you gasp for air.

You look down and see clouds below and the ragged
rocks of the mountain peak just under your feet.

Your lungs sting as you gasp for air.

You look up with wind-stung eyes to see that part of the
sky that bends from bluest blue into blackest black.

Your lungs sting as you gasp for air.

You look up, and the stars are so close they are like
streams of white ribbons holding the darkness back
from the world far below the mountaintop.

And then you hear his wise voice
and with it you can breathe again . . .

AT THE END OF ALL THINGS

YOUR FUTURE CAN BE BETTER THAN YOUR BEGINNING

he King wants to show you what waits ahead for the citizens of his kingdom—as well as what lies ahead for the serpent's slaves. For those who are the King's, there is a blessed hope; for his enemies, there is only a forever curse. Right now, you stand between what the Death Killer started and what the Death Killer will complete. The kingdom is small today, but soon it will cover everything the King has made.

What you are about to see is what will happen at the end when the King wins, he conquers his enemies, and he makes his world better than when it began. But, like those traveling through a storm to get to paradise, you must first face the consequences of a world torn by sin before you can see the perfect plans he has for his creation.

THE COMING GRAVE

We begin where you will end first. Death waits at the end of everyone's life, including yours. But it doesn't mean the King is done with his image bearers. There is more work to be done, especially for those who belong to the Death Killer. Maybe you've heard about death's ways or maybe you've even met death in your own life. Death makes a mess of things, because death is friends with sin. It helps make up the poison the serpent injected into the world so long ago. It is a part of God's just and right judgment against sinners, which is why it looms like a dark cloud on your life's horizon.

Death tries to break the King's design for you by snapping the unity between the image bearer's body and soul. Death sends the body to the grave and the soul into what those in your world might call the "in-between." That's because your soul is unbreakable; the soul does not go into the grave.

THE IN-BETWEEN

Instead, after death, the soul stands on this side of the grave separated from the body waiting for its new and better body to come. What happens in the in-between depends on who has your allegiance. If you belong to the Death Killer, then you enter immediately into heaven and the presence of your King. If you carry the mark of the serpent, then your soul plunges headlong into Hades, the place of unbearable torment and despair. In the in-between, the mix of good and bad, love and pain, that we know so well in this world is gone. Those who are with the King know only the good, true, and beautiful while those who serve the serpent feel only the bad, false, and ugly. Up ahead, it is all or nothing. You either stand in the warm light of the King's love or you suffer in the hopeless heartache of the serpent's hateful sting.

THE RESURRECTION FOR ALL

Yet the in-between is not the end; that is why it's called the in-between. A reunion is coming, one the Death Killer showed us long ago. Do you remember the empty tomb? On the other side of the in-between is a resurrection—a promise that you will know life again as body and soul. What sin and death broke, the King fixes and makes even better than before. Bodies that were once weak, lowly, embarrassing, and slowly falling apart, the King re-creates into bodies that will finally and fully be strong, glorious, honorable, and perfect.

The King is not done with you. Death does not win. That is why the Son is the Death Killer. It is why there is an empty tomb. After a short time of the soul being away from the body, the King will bring his design back together—this time with more glory and perfection, especially for his faith-filled ones.

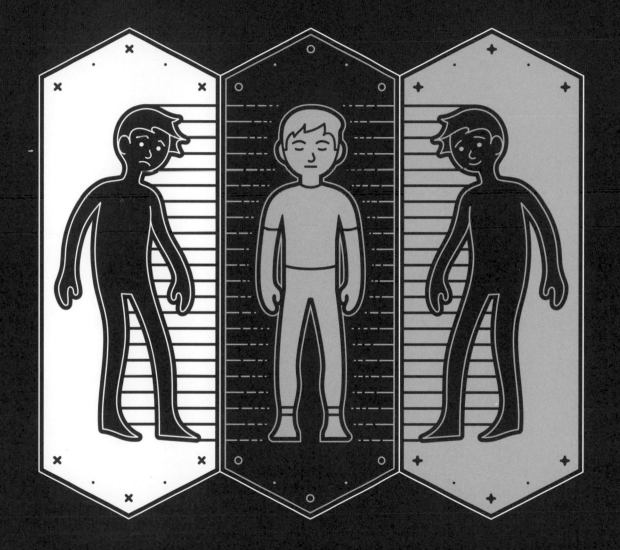

THE DEATH KILLER RETURNS

The resurrection waits for the Death Killer's second coming. Remember, the King is not finished. The Son will return to his world in the same way as he left it at his ascension. It will be a personal, incarnational, visible, glorious, and victorious homecoming. He comes a second time, not to deal with sin, but to conquer and usher in the King's promises in full. He comes not with a cross this time, but with a sword in order to make everything right for those who are waiting for him. And though the King freely gives you this promise, he does not offer you the specific time of his Death Killer's return. But the promise is enough to keep your eyes open to his coming and your hearts pure for his arrival when he brings glory and justice.

THE LAST JUDGMENT

But before the King starts your world's new beginning at your world's end, he promises one final judgment. From his great throne—the one you saw across the crystal glass sea—the Death Killer will judge the trust, loyalty, and love of every single image bearer based on the works that flow out of each person's faith. The Son will announce to the onlooking cosmos who belongs to him and who belongs to the enemy. And then he will pour out his full wrath upon the serpent and the faithless, turning hell into the lake of fire where all who oppose the King will suffer misery, pain, and torment forever. If you stand against the Death Killer, you face an eternity without hope. Without the King. Without peace. Without love. Without end.

ALL THINGS NEW

But for those who belong to the Death Killer, he has taken this wrath and punishment on himself. You don't have to face it because he already faced it for you and made a way for you to spend forever before his glorious and grace-filled face. Not only do you have him—which is and will forever be enough—but he keeps giving you more and more, with completed promises upon completed promises. He makes you a part of his people. He gives you a place where you can rest and rejoice. He gives you his presence without limit and without end.

He does this all with the new heavens and new earth. To see it, just look up.

And there coming down out of heaven almost within reach of the mountain peak, is a heavenly city. But it is unlike any city you've ever seen. It extends over the whole face of the restored earth. It both reflects and surpasses the image, shape, and dimension of the old city Jerusalem and, when you look closer, the very temple—without restrictions—that used to be that city's center.

It is a city adorned with gold and precious stones. It has walls without gates filled with people from every corner of the earth and every year of earth's old calendar. Still, the city has a garden-like beauty to it. That is because a river of life, like those that bordered Eden long ago, now flows from the throne where the King rightfully sits, robed in brilliant light.

And then a new and better voice—a regal and powerful one—speaks from the throne, shaking the mountain and the recreated world with these glorious and perfect words:

> *"Behold, the dwelling place of God is with man. He will dwell with them, and they will be his people, and God himself will be with them as their God. He will wipe away every tear from their eyes, and death shall be no more, neither shall there be mourning, nor crying, nor pain anymore, for the former things have passed away." (Rev. 21:3–4)*

As things calm and settle, the same beautiful, yet imposing voice that just shook the new heavens and new earth whispers, like he was right next to you, this promise:

"Behold, I am making all things new" (Rev. 21:5).

You turn, hoping to see the King.

But he is not there.

Instead, all you see is a faint shadow of someone you vaguely recognize. He stands for a moment and then asks you in that all too familiar and wise voice the question you've been asking yourself ever since you met him:

"Do you want him to make you new?"

As he asks the question, you finally see the messenger sent by the King to lead you on this glorious journey. The Key Keeper now stands before you shrouded in an unbearable light all his own. You freeze up when you see him, while a wave of fear and guilt swells in your heart. Why didn't you ever ask? Why didn't you ever look him in the eye? How could you have missed his excellence like this?

To fix your mistake, you bow your head. You prepare your apology in your mind as you kneel before him. To make up for it, you will sing of his honor and praise his splendor.

But before you can say anything, he powerfully warns you.

"You must not do that. I am a fellow servant with you and with those who keep the words of the King," he thunders.

As he speaks these words, the mountain melts into the now familiar sea of crystal and you find yourself on the near shore, in the shadow of the thrones and the scroll with the unbroken seals.

This time you are not alone. Before you are four strange and majestic creatures, singing the deep words you first heard in the King's heavenly throne room here on this new earth.

> *Holy, holy, holy, is the Lord God Almighty, who was and is and is to come! (Rev. 4:8)*

Then the twenty-four elders march before the greatest throne, throw down their crowns, fall on their faces, and begin their own song:

> *Worthy are you, our Lord and God,*
> *to receive glory and honor and power,*
> *for you created all things,*
> *and by your will they existed and were created. (Rev. 4:11)*

"Who is worthy to open the scroll? Who is worthy to break the seals? Is there anyone from heaven? Is there one from earth?" they ask and ask and ask.

But no one comes.

Sadness builds up in your heart until you hear the Key Keeper say, "Worship *him*, instead."

That's when you hear the sound. It drives back your sadness like a fire melts the snow. It is the sound you've longed to hear since you first heard it. It is the beautifully mysterious mixture of a lamb's bleat and a lion's roar.

Then you see him. The Lion of the Tribe of Judah who is also the Lamb of God. He is the one you've longed to see. He is the Death Killer who boldly and humbly stands with the scroll in his hand.

The chorus of elders and creatures sing a new song to the Lamb:

> *Worthy are you to take the scroll*
> *and to open its seals,*
> *for you were slain, and by your blood you ransomed people for God*
> *from every tribe and language and people and nation,*
> *and you have made them a kingdom and priests to our God,*
> *and they shall reign on the earth. (Rev. 5:9–10)*

Then countless angels, who look and sound like your Key Keeper, gather before the Death Killer's throne and sing in perfect harmony,

> *Worthy is the Lamb who was slain,*
> *to receive power and wealth and wisdom and might*
> *and honor and glory and blessing! (Rev. 5:12)*

Everything that the King ever made—every creature in heaven and on earth and under the earth and in the sea, and all that is in them—including you—sing with unequaled beauty:

> *To him who sits on the throne and to the Lamb*
> *be blessing and honor and glory and might forever and ever! (Rev. 5:13)*

And the world stands still. Everything goes quiet. All of creation worships the Lion, the Lamb, the Death Killer, not only in song, but also in thought, action, and every part of their lives.

In the deep quiet, you can hear the scroll's seals break and the parchment unfurl.

Everything goes black.

Except for you, the Death Killer, and the scroll.

What does it say? Is your name inside? Will he make everything right? These thoughts scramble through your head, but you can't look away from the Lamb.

He holds out the scroll. You inch toward it to see what fearful grace and mercy it holds. Everything you've ever known and not known and wanted to know flashes across the scroll. Names upon names upon names fill the parchment, but somehow they all flow together into one simple and beautiful name.

Jesus.

Then the parchment goes blank.

And the Death Killer speaks these words onto the page:

"Come."

And then, "Surely, I am coming soon."

Like the words on the scroll, the Lamb vanishes. The unsealed scroll flutters to the ground and lands beside a book with a key on top of it. Attached with a string is a small note of instruction that reads:

You turned the key to open the lock, and now
you aren't the same;
You've seen your deepest guilt and faced
your darkest shame.
You now know what he made you to be and what
you're supposed to become,
but still you need to hold the key because
your story remains undone.

You hear the wise and familiar voice of the Key Keeper one last time.

"To find your way back here again, use this key to unlock this book. It is the King's speech. It is his perfect instructions on how to find your way back to the Lion and the Lamb."

Turn the key, open the book, and fall in love with your King.

OPEN THE BOOK
Where to Turn the Key in Your Bible

This book was written *for you*. It was written to show you the beautiful story of God's work in God's world for the worship of God. Yet, while this book tells an epic tale, it is only a faint whisper of a better story—the story God wrote to you himself. So let this book be what it was meant to be: an *introduction* to the even bigger epic in your Bible and an *invitation* to open and find your story in the pages of God's story. So, if you find the courage to open your Bible, you can find many of the keys to knowing God in the passages below.